THE PRINCETON REVIEW

STUDENT ADVANTAGE GUIDE TO

SUMMER

1996 EDITION

Books in The Princeton Review Series
Cracking the ACT
Cracking the ACT with Sample Tests on Computer Disk
Cracking the GED
Cracking the GMAT
Cracking the GMAT with Sample Tests on Computer Disk
Cracking the GRE
Cracking the GRE with Sample Tests on Computer Disk
Cracking the GRE Psychology Subject Test
Cracking the LSAT
Cracking the LSAT with Sample Tests on Computer Disk
Cracking the MCAT
Cracking the MCAT with Sample Tests on Computer Disk
Cracking the SAT and PSAT
Cracking the SAT and PSAT with Sample Tests on Computer Disk
Cracking the SAT II: Biology Subject Test
Cracking the SAT II: Chemistry Subject Test
Cracking the SAT II: English Subject Tests
Cracking the SAT II: French Subject Test
Cracking the SAT II: History Subject Tests
Cracking the SAT II: Math Subject Tests
Cracking the SAT II: Physics Subject Test
Cracking the SAT II: Spanish Subject Test
Cracking the TOEFL with Audiocassette

Culturescope
Culturescope Elementary
Culturescope High School

SAT Math Workout
SAT Verbal Workout

Don't Be a Chump!
How to Survive Without Your Parents' Money
Speak Now!
Trashproof Resumes

Grammar Smart
Math Smart
Reading Smart
Study Smart
Word Smart: Building an Educated Vocabulary
Word Smart II: How to Build a More Educated Vocabulary
Word Smart Executive
Word Smart Genius
Writing Smart

Grammar Smart Junior
Math Smart Junior
Word Smart Junior
Writing Smart Junior

Business School Companion
Law School Companion

Student Access Guide to America's Top Internships
Student Access Guide to College Admissions
Student Access Guide to the Best Business Schools
Student Access Guide to the Best Law Schools
Student Access Guide to the Best Medical Schools
Student Access Guide to the Best 309 Colleges
Student Access Guide to Paying for College
Student Access Guide: The Big Book of Colleges
Student Access Guide: The Internship Bible
Student Advantage Guide to Summer
Student Advantage Guide to Visiting College Campuses

Also available on cassette from Living Language
Grammar Smart
Word Smart
Word Smart II

THE PRINCETON REVIEW

STUDENT ADVANTAGE GUIDE TO

SUMMER

1996 EDITION

BY MICHAEL FREEDMAN

Random House, Inc.   New York   1995

Princeton Review Publishing, L.L.C.
2315 Broadway, 3rd Floor
New York, NY 10024
e-mail: info@review.com

ISBN 0-679-76470-4

Edited by Amy E. Zavatto
Designed by Dinica Quesada
Illustrations by John Bergdahl and Michael Recorvits

Manufactures in the United States of America on partially recycled paper.
98765432
First Edition

Contents

ACKNOWLEDGMENTS

The author would like to acknowledge Howie Fox, Beverly Schiffman, David Schaller, and Meryl Glasser whose expertise helped make this book a reality. He'd also like to thank John Katzman, Amy Zavatto, PJ Waters, Lee Elliott, Chris Kensler, Doug McMullen, Bruno Blumenfeld, and Maria Russo for their excellent ideas and editing skills. In addition, thank you to all who have shared their experiences in the book and to Jonathon and Jo Freedman for making everything possible.

Introduction

For eight-and-a-half months out of the year you're a slave to book reports, exams, parents, teachers, coaches, and schedules. In short, you're a pretty busy person. And you definitely don't need to be in AP math to figure out that only two-and-a-half months of summer is not a whole lot of time. Now, we know you're pretty smart and can probably find *something* to do from Memorial Day to Labor Day, but a few suggestions can't hurt. So here you have it—*The Princeton Review's Student Access Guide to Summer*. This isn't a schedule or a manual or even a how-to book. It's just some good info on how to make your summer the best one possible—no matter what you want to do.

The Guide to Summer will show you the many opportunities open to you during summer vacation. You can:

> *Start your own business*
>
> *Work at an exciting summer job*
>
> *Help build huts in Africa*
>
> *Go to tennis camp in Florida*
>
> *Bike around New England, France, Colorado, or Ireland*
>
> *Write the next great novel*
>
> *Learn how to use a computer*
>
> *Learn to speak Japanese*
>
> *Go white-water rafting in Wyoming*
>
> *Prep for your PSATs/SATs*
>
> *Teach underprivileged kids how to read*
>
> *See the Grand Canyon*

Were you reading that list and saying to yourself, "No way, I'll never be able to do that." Well, of course you can't do everything, but chances are there are a few things that are not only possible, but that you might not even have thought of before. Beware, though; many of the best things to do over the summer require an early start. Getting a great summer job is much easier if you start looking in March, and many of the programs listed in this book fill up quickly, so you should start your search as soon as possible.

Hanging Out

Even if you go on one of the great programs listed in the book, you'll still have plenty of time to kick around the house. The longest of the travel programs is only six weeks, and the shorter (and cheaper) programs sometimes last only one week. This means that no matter what you do or where you go, you'll still have time to hang out. If you don't travel, there are a zillion things you can do locally—even in your own home. In every section of the book, we've given you tons of ideas. After all, you can cover a lot of territory in two-and-a-half months.

Working

Many of you will need to earn money this summer, but sometimes, it's hard to find a good summer job. The competition is intense, but if you know the ins and outs, you'll be able to find meaningful, well-paying work. We'll show you the best way to find a *good* summer job, as well as how to network and have a successful interview. We'll even give you a few pointers on how to start your own business.

Going Places

Summer is a time to do cool things like traveling or enrolling in a summer program. We've checked out hundreds of summer programs, and we've listed the best.

Experiment

Do something that you might not get the chance to do during the regular school year. Take some chances. This is the time to try something that you've never done before or to go somewhere you never thought you'd go.

When Should You Be Reading This Book?

It might be tempting to wait until June to plan your summer, but you might miss a lot of opportunities. Many of the programs that we describe in this book require you to apply early. And of course, the earlier you look for a job the better. A good time to start planning for next summer is this winter. This will give you plenty of time to sift through the options and plan the perfect summer. If you're getting a late start, though, don't worry. We have designed this book so that no matter when you read it, you'll find things to do this summer.

Why This Book?

There are a number of books that list various summer programs and camps, but often these books are directed at your parents—*they* get to decide what *you* do for the summer. We at The Princeton Review unanimously agreed that what you do should be *your* choice. So, we give you options. We'll talk about what you can do if you can't afford to go on a trip to Kathmandu. We'll help you pick out some of the best summer programs around, show you how to find jobs, and give you cool things to do if you're just hanging out. *The Guide to Summer* has everything, from working at Mickey Dees to checking out the streets of Zanzibar.

How We Chose the Programs

You might wonder how we decided which programs to include in this book. We asked hundreds of high school students what programs they have enjoyed, because we wanted to find the ones that are fun and educational. We also tried to give you as much variety as possible. There are programs in *The Guide* that will take you almost anywhere on the globe. You can perform community services, go to camp, or see the world.

For each of the major programs, we interviewed students who participated and found out the inside scoop, so you'll know what you're getting into. Then we talked to the best camp advisory services in the country. These services send people to the programs, and continually review the quality through student surveys. Using all this research, we have determined which programs are exciting, well run, and professional.

The Symbols

In addition, we've included a unique Princeton Review graphic system for getting info on all the activities in the book at a glance. Everything we list in the book is worth a look, but you'll have to find out which activities are for you. For example, if you know you like to take showers every day, you won't want to go to a program where you only get one a month.

Here's the system:

Who Sets the Agenda

Some of the programs we list will do most of the planning for you (right icon). Others might provide you with a backdrop, but will require you to get out there and figure things out on your own (left icon). And then there are still others that will be a little bit of both (center icon).

Costs

Most of the programs require some sort of fee. They range from expensive (left icon) to middle of the road (center icon) to fairly reasonable (right icon).

Zoom In, Zoom Out

Depending on how much territory you're looking to cover over the summer months, some activities will focus on a particular area of the world (right icon), some will cover more than one place (middle icon), and others will bring you to several different locations (left icon).

Intellectual or Physical

If you're looking to really get a good workout this summer, look for the programs that indicates lots of physical activity (right icon). Maybe you don't want to be the poster youth for "Abs of Steel," but would like to have some physical activity tied in with a bit of thought-provoking activity as well (center icon). Or perhaps you're really looking for some intense brain activity. If so, look for the programs and activities that indicate heavy thinking (left icon).

Stylin'

There are those of us who would choose a sleeping bag and stars over a comfy couch with remote controlled TV propped in front of it any day (left icon), while others would absolutely go nuts without access to cable (right icon). Some people just need a clean bed and a shower to be happy (center icon).

Be In Next Year's Edition

We're always looking for people who did cool things over the summer. If you did something worthwhile that's not in the book, send us a card with a description of what you did and your phone number. We may use your idea in next year's edition. Send to:

The Princeton Review
2315 Broadway 3rd Floor
New York, NY 10024
Attn: Publishing/Summer Book

Hanging Out

THE TRUTH ABOUT SUMMER

When it comes right down to it, you'll probably be spending most of your summer chilling out. That's what summers are for. Even the organized activities presented later in the book—the jobs, the programs, the sports—only take up part of your summer.

So, what are you going to do with all that extra time on your hands? We're pretty sure you've got some ideas, but we'd like to make some suggestions.

Does this sound familiar? On the first day of summer you decide to sit in the sun. You put on some shades, grab your Walkman, pour yourself a lemonade from the fridge, and set out a lawn chair. It's a beautiful day, but after about 10 minutes, you realize that *there is nothing to do*. So you call your friends, they come over, and then you all hang out together. After an hour of wondering if so-and-so is still dating so-and-so, someone asks, "Is this all we're gonna do this summer—hang out?"

Well, you can. You can do whatever you want, but you'll have more fun if you do something more with your vacation. We're going to suggest some stuff to do with your free time, things that will enrich your mind and body and maybe even help you get into the college of your choice.

You see, you can spend your entire summer vegging out and start the next year exactly where you left off. Or you can do something with your time. You will be surprised at just how much you can accomplish when you don't have school.

You Are in Control

Take an active part in planning your summer. Even if you don't want to work and can't go on some fancy program, there are still many good things that you can do without even traveling away from home. And even if you do get a job *and* go on a program, there's still going to be time left to do your own thing.

The first step is to get going. If you wait patiently for something exciting to happen, it won't. The whole summer will pass you by. The only way to enjoy your summer is to reach out and grab it by the nose. Make plans; call people; go on a day trip; enjoy yourself. In other words, get off your butt and do something.

Sometimes the best summers can be found through your own initiative. Vanessa Ho of New York City did a variety of things over the summer before she entered tenth grade. She started by working as a clerk during the day and taking ballet classes in the evening. This lasted for a few weeks.

"Then I went to Scotland and visited relatives for a week. I flew a plane with an instructor. My uncle flies planes, and he thought it would be fun for me to try, so we set up a flying lesson. It wasn't scary. It was a two-person plane with dual controls. The instructor took off and landed, but when we were in the air, I could move around and turn.

"While I was in Scotland, I also rode horses and shopped and stuff. Then, my family and I took a trip to Maine and Martha's Vineyard and Boston and visited relatives. It was a great summer."

Summer Dos and Don'ts

No matter what you do, no matter where you're from, no matter how good a student you are, there are some things that you should never do on your summer vacation.

Don't Watch Bad TV

It's all reruns. If you find you're beginning to resemble the color of certain types of fungi, you're spending too much time with Oprah. We can't begin to tell you how many summers have been ruined by talk shows and MTV. Choose what shows you watch carefully or, better yet, don't watch TV at all. It's summer, after all, and the sun is shining; don't be a couch potato.

Don't Look Bored

Don't tell your parents that you're bored. They'll most likely find some awful chore for you to do. If you don't believe us, give it a try, but be prepared to spend the next few days cleaning out that scary cabinet underneath the sink or giving the dog a flea dip.

Don't Sleep Much Past Noon

Well, at least not on the weekends. Everyone and their brother is rolling out of bed at noon on Saturday and Sunday, and, although they don't mean it, they're blocking your way to the beach. You don't have to get up early for school during the summer, but you should still get out of bed to face the day. If you wake up at two in the afternoon, most of the day will be gone, and your summer will pass you by.

Do Become Involved

There's great stuff out there to see and do, so don't sit back and wait for them to happen—take control and make decisions.

Do Try to Learn Something

Just because school's out is no reason to shut off your mind. Instead of learning the concrete curriculum, teach yourself something totally off the roster. Summer is a great time to take control of your education and to learn things that you're interested in at your own pace. Check out our chapter on enriching your mind on pages 89-119.

If You're Going to Work a Job, Do it Right

We all need money, but it doesn't necessarily have to be a drag to get it. If you have to work, find an interesting job. Read our chapter entitled Working (pages 13-46), and then find a job that challenges you and teaches you something. If you do get a job, do it well. No matter how boring the work is, the time will go faster and you'll feel better about yourself if you work to the best of your ability. And you'll be able to get a good college recommendation from your employer.

Do At Least One Thing That You've Never Done Before

Experiment. Do something great. It could be something as simple as joining your local community theater, volunteering to spend some time with senior citizens, or maybe finding some quiet spot to sit down and work on that short story or poem you've been mulling over for a while. The beauty of it is you're making your own agenda—you can do a different thing every week or every month or commit yourself to one activity the entire vacation. Nobody's telling you what to do, so go crazy.

2

Working

HOW TO GET A GOOD SUMMER JOB

Start early. If you already have a part-time job you like, see if there's some possibility for working more hours over the summer. If you don't work during the school year, start looking by about April or May. Finding a job is hard work, but if you follow our advice you'll be taking home a paycheck in no time.

A summer job is a great opportunity to learn new things. Don't worry about stuff like what you want to do with your life, because any job will teach you some skills you'll need later on when you are not in school anymore. Also, summer jobs sometimes lead to full-time work after you finish school. We know a few people who started their careers at companies that were so happy with the students' work, they kept asking them back summer after summer. Eventually, the companies hired the students full time after college. At the very least, you can sling hash with some new friends.

The Bad News

Let's face it, you're not going to get rich over the summer. Most jobs that you can get as a high school student pay minimum wage or, if you're lucky, a few pennies more. (The average hourly wage for high school students was $4.73 an hour when we went to press. Ninety-two percent of students made less than $6.00 an hour. [Source: Bureau of Labor and Statistics Employment in Perspective: Work Activity of Students]) Not only is the pay pretty sketchy, but you'll probably face stiff competition for these jobs, and knowing some the tricks to finding a good one can't hurt.

The Good News

This is not to say that you should give up before you start. On the contrary, there are a lot of great opportunities for summer employment out there. One thing you can count on: employers today, no matter what they pay, are all looking for responsible people who show up on time, ready to work. And the skills that employers want can be picked up by working any job over the summer.

You *can* make some decent cash. A summer spent working for minimum wage could leave you with $1,500 for spending money over the year. Some jobs pay even more. And then during the school year, when it comes time to borrow the car for a concert, you can offer to throw in some gas when your parents are hesitant.

There are other benefits to getting a job. The experience of seeking a job is good practice. According to the U.S. Department of Labor, you will most likely have to shift careers four times in your life. The sooner you learn how to get a job, the better. Also, summer employment is a great way to meet people. Working a job will introduce you to other high school students who don't go to your school and whom you probably wouldn't get the chance to meet during the year.

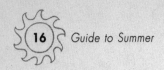

Networking

One of the best ways to find a job is by networking: using your connections to meet the right people to get you started. It can be hard to find a good summer job, so you need all the help you can get. Without using connections, it's hard to know what's out there.

What connections, you say? A connection is somebody you know who might be willing to help you. That's it. You don't need to know the president of MTV to find a fun, decent-paying job. You'll be surprised to see how many people will go out of their way for you. Just to give you an idea, we'll start with the best connections you have: your parents. Most likely they have jobs and know a lot of other people who have jobs.

How about the friend of your aunt who owns a restaurant? Or your neighbor with the dog-walking business? Even if you run across employers who don't usually hire high school students, maybe you can convince them that you're the right person for the job.

If your parents can't help you out, check out the guidance counselor's office. Many employers who want to hire high school students contact guidance counselors to list any open positions.

 Geoff Martz of Detroit, Michigan spent the summer before his senior year working for a photographer in Paris: "It was a studio where they did a whole bunch of different things. Once a month they did all the layouts for Lui (Him), the Playboy of France. I got the job through a lawyer who was a vague friend of my father's. The summer before I had worked in his office filing. He liked me and said, 'you should do something interesting this summer.'"

One vivid memory for Martz is the night they took the photographs for a clothing designer: "It was really wild. The clothes arrived in an armored truck because they didn't want anybody to steal the fashion ideas. The models would change in the armored truck and then jump into the studio for fifteen minutes. There were guys with guns and the whole thing was done at night."

Martz advises that when you get a summer job to have a positive attitude: "I had a really bad attitude in the beginning. When they asked me to get coffee, I was insulted: "Why should I be getting coffee; I'm smarter than that." As the summer went on and my attitude improved, they let me do other things. Everyone has to do shit-work; even your boss has to do it."

With networking, the more people you ask, the better. Talk to your friends, your teachers, and anybody who knows you or might know of a job. In addition to asking at home and around school, you might want to ask in places where teenagers are usually working. For example, go to a fast-food place and ask to speak to the manager. The turnover in fast-food is rapid, which means that they're always looking for new people. If you come in at the right time, you may find that they're hiring.

Robin Newgate of Atlantic City, New Jersey got a lucrative summer job through connections. She worked at a casino: "There was a chair concession outside of the casinos. Guests came by, showed me their room key, and I brought these big heavy chairs down to the beach for them and they tipped me. At the end of the day, we gathered the chairs up. In the middle of the day, we got to work on our tans. I got paid ten bucks an hour plus seventy or eighty dollars a day in tips."

She got the job through her father: "We lived next door to the people who owned the casino. All the people who got the job were connected, but you didn't have to know the owner. You could have known someone in the health club."

Working at a casino gave Newgate some insight into gamblers and life in general: "It was very interesting at the time, but it drove me nuts. I was ready to go to college and all these gamblers would talk about what they won. They never talked about what they lost, but what they won was more than I was going to end up paying for college for four years. That was always really blowing my mind. One guy who had been gambling all day and who'd forgotten what money meant gave me 100 dollars. Those people were nuts. All the ladies had two sets of jewelry, one real set and one faux set that exactly matched their real jewelry for the beach. It was crazy. They were gross people."

While her job was profitable, Newgate admits that it wasn't easy: "It was better than waiting tables. I mean, you can get a job working in the florist office or waiting tables. I'd pick the florist office."

The classified ads in the newspaper will sometimes lead to work, but a job hunt through the paper can be frustrating. Read through the ads and carefully look for employers who might hire high school students. And be aware that some of the ads are not legitimate. If an ad sounds too good ($20 an hour, no experience necessary), it's probably a scam. Don't apply for a job if you have to pay for something. If they need employees, they will pay you, not the other way around.

WHAT KINDS OF JOBS ARE THERE?

We went through piles of government data to figure out which employers generally hire in the summer. Over the last three years, the following categories have yielded an average of 1,450,000 summer jobs a year [Source: Bureau of Labor and Statistics]. Be confident: there is a job out there for you.

Amusement and Recreation (320,000 jobs)

There are tons of jobs at places like movie theaters, beaches, amusement parks, and miniature golf courses. Because more people have free time in the summer, new employees are needed to handle the extra business. You might be able to work outside, and you can definitely have a good time hanging out after work.

You might wonder where to find a job like this. If you happen to live in a touristy city like Orlando, the answer is easy. Ask yourself where all the tourists go. That's where you'll find the jobs. In Orlando, as you might guess, Disney is always hiring high school students.

In most places, however, you won't find one place that hires thousands of high school students. You'll have to scout out places that have entertainment jobs. Look for bowling alleys, pools, country clubs, or baseball stadiums. These places will need new employees over the summer.

Eating and Drinking (308,000 jobs)

More people eat out over the summer. There are usually two kinds of pay for these jobs. If you work at a fast-food place or in the kitchen of a restaurant, you'll most likely get minimum wage, but if you can get a waiter or waitress job, you can earn a lot of money in tips.

Good places for getting a job right away are in the national chains: McDonald's, Burger King, Pizza Hut, Taco Bell, etc. They love to hire high school students. But, look for family-owned restaurants too, especially if you live in an area that gets a lot of tourists from Memorial Day to Labor Day. You may be able to earn more money and work in an intimate setting.

Also try seasonal businesses like concession stands or ice cream trucks. Finally, a great place to look for work is catering services. Caterers do a lot more business over the summer, and the work can be really fun with good pay.

Hotels (164,000 jobs)

Since many people travel in the summer, hotels need more workers. In addition to clerk, porter, and chambermaid jobs, some hotels and inns serve food as well and might need wait and kitchen staff. Look in your local yellow pages. Check the national companies like Hyatt and any local hotels. Chances are you'll find someone looking for help.

Food and Kindred Products (57,000 jobs)

Supermarkets also hire more people for the summer, so it's a good place to seek out a job. Again, the best way is to check out the phone book. Look for a place near your home, and call or go in to introduce yourself to the manager to see if there are any openings.

Construction (473,000 jobs)

Construction jobs hire a lot of people for the summer. Even though many are looking for skilled labor, there are a lot of unskilled jobs as well. Be ready to work hard. The work may be strenuous, but you will probably be paid well. In addition to work in the field, construction companies need office people. Look in the phone book for contractors and builders.

Farming (96,000 jobs)

If you live in an area where there are a lot of farms, you can often help out with planting and harvesting. These jobs can be hard physical work, but they're outside and you can learn stuff about growing fruits and vegetables.

Real Estate (73,000 jobs)

When the weather turns warm, people start looking for houses. This means that there are more jobs for people in real estate offices. Try calling some local offices— they just might need someone for fielding calls and filing papers.

YOU'RE GETTING COLDER

You may be looking in the wrong place. Many high school students go to the mall and fill out applications at every store. While convenient (the stores are right next to each other), the mall is not a good place to find summer jobs. The following employers got rid of employees during the last few years:

- *clothing stores*
- *furniture stores*
- *general merchandise stores (Wal-Mart, Kmart, Target, etc.)*
- *department stores*
- *day-care centers*

SUMMER JOBS THAT PAY MORE THAN MINIMUM WAGE

There are certain jobs that have generally paid high school students good money. Although they are sometimes hard to get or require specific skills, these jobs can help you earn more money than most high school students do over the summer.

Lifeguard

If you know how to swim, take a few months' training and get certified as a lifeguard. The pay is good, you can get a great tan, and you can be around your friends. Start with your local recreation department to find out the requirements.

Caddie

If you live near a golf course, see if you can be a caddie. You get tips, you're outside in a nice setting, and sometimes the course lets you play a round of golf free.

Waiting Tables

Because you get tips, waiting tables can be a good deal. The work is hard, but you really can make a lot of money (and meet some pretty interesting people). Since customers tip a percentage of the bill, you might make more money at an expensive restaurant. However, the more expensive the restaurant is, generally the more professional-looking and experienced you'll need to be to get the job.

Catering

Although not all catering jobs pay more than minimum wage, some do. The work is similar to waiting tables, but you won't get tips. The hourly wage, however, is usually more. Look in your yellow pages for caterers. Call them to see if they have jobs available. Then go and apply.

Parking Cars at Events and Restaurants

If you have your driver's license, you might be able to get a job parking cars. At some events, a person drives her car to the front door. A runner gets in the car, parks it, then runs back and waits for the next car. The work is intense (lots of running), but when you retrieve the car, the owner will usually tip you. Besides, you get to drive some nice cars that you might never get to drive again.

Computer Work

If you learn how to use some of the popular computer programs and you live near or in a city, you can get a job working with a computer. Either by taking a class or through studying on your own, learn how to type and then learn at least one of the following programs:

> ***Word processing programs*** *Word for Windows, WordPerfect for Windows*
>
> ***Layout programs*** *Powerpoint, QuarkXPress, Illustrator, Pagemaker*

In some cities, the easiest way to get a computer job is through a temp agency, but as a high school student, you may have to go directly to the companies. Look for places like banks or publishers who would need layout work. Call big corporations in your area and offer your services. If you can find the work, the experience will help out down the road.

SUMMER JOBS THAT ARE FUN

Some jobs are just more fun than others. They may not pay much, but who cares?

Working at a Ballpark

If you have a baseball team in your area, call in March and try to get a job at the stadium. You'll be outside (unless there's a dome), and you'll get to see crowds of people every day. It can be a great way to spend the summer.

Working at Camp

If you're seventeen or eighteen and have gone to camp for a few years, there's a good chance you may be able to get a job as a camp counselor. Check out pages 31-32.

Working at a Beach or Pool

Even if you can't swim, you can get a job near the water. Some pools and beaches have concession stands, or need people to take admission fees. Although the work might be boring, you'll be able to hang out at the pool or beach before and after work.

Any Type of Volunteer Work

Although this work won't pay much (if anything at all), you'll feel great helping other people. See pages 39-41 for volunteer opportunities.

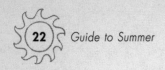

CREATE YOUR OWN POSITION

Although certain employers are always hiring high school students, many may not know that they even need you. If you can get in touch with the boss and explain how good a worker you are, you might be able to create your own job. Most employers are looking for dedicated workers. If you can show someone how great you are, you can convince an employer that you should get a job. Here's how to do it:

Step 1. Pick Your Targets

What are you interested in? Do you want to do something with science or math? Do you want to work in publishing or maybe in graphic design? Pick the type of job you might like and then find local businesses that do that type of work. Make a list of companies and small businesses in the field you want to enter.

Step 2. Research Your Targets

Call or visit the companies; find out exactly what kind of work they do. Check out your local library for background info. Find out who the boss is.

Step 3. Contact Your Targets

Call or write a letter expressing how much you want the job. You want the employer to feel that you'll be a great worker, an asset to the company, but that you won't complain or require too much supervision (i.e., time out of his or her busy day). Be sure to point out:

- *how interested you are in the type of work*
- *how impressed you are with the company*
- *how great a worker you'll be*
- *that you'll work cheap (optional)*

Here's a sample letter:

Joe Bloggs
123 Main Street
Anywhere, U.S. 12345
Date

ACME Publishing
226 Washington Blvd.

Dear Ms. Smith,

I'm a high school student attending City High, and my lifelong dream is to work in publishing. I like to read and I am fascinated by the way books are put together. ACME Publishing, although not the biggest publishing house in town, is by far the best, and I'd like to work for you this summer.

I am a good student; I've been on the honor roll for the last two years, and I've had experience working on the high school yearbook. Last year, I headed the yearbook committee and was responsible for organizing all the photos and editing all the copy. I am a hard worker, and I'm eager and willing to do what it takes to learn more about the publishing business.

I am not looking for a high salary; I am looking for a chance to learn about what the job is like so that I can decide whether to pursue a publishing career later on.

I learn fast—you won't have to tell me twice how to do things. If you have a place for a talented young person wanting to learn the business, call me at 1-214-123-4567. You won't be disappointed.

Sincerely,

Joe Bloggs

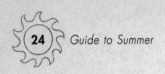

The Cold Call

Another way to create your own job is to use the phone. Just like in the letter, you want to sound passionate about the job, eager to learn, and willing to work hard. Try to get the boss on the phone. It might be hard to get through, but you'll have a much better chance of getting the job if you go to the top. Try to call a little before or after working hours. Don't give your pitch to just anybody. Chances are, they can't hire you anyway and won't be impressed by your ambition.

If you can't get through to the boss directly, call sometime when the office is closed. The company might have a voice-mail system. Practice a few times before you make the call. Make sure you leave a phone number so he can get back to you. Most important, *speak slowly*. There's nothing more annoying than having to listen to a message three times before you can translate it.

Get Out There

It's rare for high school students to call or write about jobs that don't yet exist. Most people we talked to just went from business to business in town, looking for one that was hiring. So, by making the effort, you'll stand out and have a better chance of getting a job. Most employers would be flattered to have someone show so much interest in their company, and would probably hire someone for a test period to see if she worked out.

THE APPLICATION

On application forms, you'll be asked what school you go to, what experience you have, and whom the employer should call to see if you're right for the job. Try to give this some thought ahead of time. Fill out the information as completely and honestly as you can.

The application is a good place to indicate why you'd be perfect for a particular job. If the job is to be a cashier, you might want to say how good you are in math. If it's in an office you can write something about how well you work with people. If the application has no space for any of this stuff, be sure to mention it in the interview.

 Rachel March of Altamonte Springs, Florida got a job in a Hallmark shop: "There was a 'Help Wanted' sign in the window, but the job was for someone over eighteen and I wasn't. I figured, 'It's a Hallmark shop. What could it have in it that I couldn't do?' I thought the requirement was stupid, so I didn't feel guilty about lying. I told them I was in community college and living with my family. I kept my birthday, but I just changed the year." If you work in a Hallmark shop, you've got to know when your birthday is, or you'll be getting cards on the wrong day.

Because lying got her the job, there were consequences: "The main thing was that once I started the lie, I always had to worry about getting caught. I also had to create more lies—like what my major was and what kind of job I wanted after college. I think they suspected something, but I was so good at my job that they never confronted me. They never said anything."

If you're in a situation where you think you need to lie to get a job, March advises to think twice about it. "You can't get too close to the people you work with. You have to keep a distance. You have to be careful about what you say. When I lied to get the job, I didn't realize how long I'd have to keep the lie going. There was one girl I was kind of friends with, but I had to keep lying to her, and that was kind of weird."

THE JOB INTERVIEW

Even if a potential employer likes your application, you'll probably still have to go through an interview. Don't worry, though. An interview is a great chance to show an employer why you're better for the job than all the other bozos who applied. If you can get the hang of the interview process, you'll find it useful for the many jobs you apply to later in life. Here are some hints:

Be Prepared

Take some time to do research on the business in which you might be working. If it's a store, find out what they sell and how they sell it. If you notice that they're very considerate to their customers, you can bring this up at the interview: "I noticed that you treat your customers well. I like working with people, and I would be great at making them feel comfortable." If it's some kind of big company, do research in the library and make sure you know what the company does. The person interviewing you will be much more impressed if you've done your homework. Besides, interviewers, just like everyone else, are flattered when a person knows something about what they do and where they work.

Find Out What to Wear

Ask if there's a dress code or visit the place to see what the person doing the job you're applying for is wearing. It's important to look neat and well-dressed for the interview. It doesn't matter what the job is—even if you'll be hauling pig slop. You should look responsible at the interview.

Practice

Most interviews are fairly predictable. There are a certain number of questions that they will ask you. Get your friends or your parents to practice with you.

APPEARANCE CHECKLIST

Hair washed and combed

No bad smells emanating from anywhere on your body

No overpowering good smells emanating from anywhere on your body

Freshly ironed clothes

Shoes shined

Matching socks

Matching earrings

A minimum of makeup

From *How to Survive Without Your Parents' Money*, p.103

Sell Yourself

It's not enough to just show up at an interview and seem presentable. You've got to convince the interviewer that you will make a valuable addition to the company. When you practice answering the questions, practice turning each question to your advantage. Let's say, for example, that the interviewer asks you if you've ever handled money before, and you haven't held a job working with money. Don't just say, "No dude, I've never done that before, except when I used to steal money out of my brother's wallet—does that count?" Instead say, "Well, I haven't worked a job that required me to handle money, but I was elected school treasurer, and I get good grades in math. I'm responsible and I look forward to the challenge of dealing with the cash register."

Let's say the interviewer asks you about your previous experience and you haven't ever had a job. Don't just say, "I've never worked a day in my life." Instead, tell her of some job-like thing you've done. Make it sound like you've done some activity outside of school that required responsibility, whether it's working on the yearbook or volunteering at the hospital.

Let's say the interviewer asks you about your weaknesses. Don't tell her that you don't have any. She won't believe you and you'll come off as being stuck-up. On the other hand, don't list a bunch of faults. The trick here is to list a weakness and explain how you're working your tail off to improve yourself. How about saying something like, "I often get frustrated when I try something new and I'm not immediately great at it. But lately I've been concentrating on relaxing and taking the time to get better." or "I am afraid of meeting people for the first time and I often feel nervous, but I've been working hard to meet new people and I think I'm getting better at it."

A good interview is like a balancing act. You want to seem sure of yourself but not arrogant. Most people make the mistake of being too shy, of not listing their good qualities when given the chance. Others make the mistake of seeming too good to be true. When selling your good qualities, you have to make it believable.

Act Businesslike

Make sure to get to the interview a few minutes early. Then greet the interviewer by name and shake his hand. Look the interviewer in the eye, relax, and smile. It's important to look like you know what you're doing (even if you don't). Try to look interested and answer any questions in a straightforward, concise manner. Don't chew gum, play with your keys, or otherwise look impatient or uncomfortable.

INTERVIEW QUESTIONS

Tell me about yourself.

What are your greatest strengths/weaknesses?

How much do you expect to get paid?

Where else have you worked?

Do you like working with people?

When can you work?

Do you want to work full-time or part-time?

Have you ever worked with money on a job?

What do you bring to this job?

Are you applying anywhere else?

Why should we hire you?

Any questions?

When can you start?

Leave a Good Impression

The last steps in an interview should always be the same. Say, "Thank you, Ms. ____. I really enjoyed meeting you and finding out more about this great job." Smile, and wait for a reply. Even if the interviewer doesn't respond, finish the interview by saying, "I look forward to hearing from you."

If you follow all these instructions you'll have a successful interview, but it doesn't end there. Now it's time to take the extra step necessary to guarantee that first paycheck.

Follow Up

It's not enough to impress the interviewer. You have to remind her of your interview, too. Once you get home from the interview, write a follow-up note thanking the employer for taking the time to talk with you.

Here's a sample note:

> Joe Bloggs
> 123 Main Street
> Anywhere, U.S. 12345
>
> Minuscule Industries
> 224 Washington Blvd.
>
> Dear Ms. Smith:
> Thank you for taking the time to talk with me about the filing job at Minuscule
> Industries. I really enjoyed talking with you and am excited about working for
> the company. Please let me know if there's any more information I can give you.
> I can be reached at 123-456-7890.
>
> Sincerely,
> Joe Bloggs

In addition to a note, it's important to call. A few days after the interview, show some initiative and make a follow-up call: "Hi, this is Joe Bloggs. I interviewed for the filing job. Thank you again for spending all that time in the interview. Is there anything else I can tell you that might help you to make a decision? I just wanted to say how much I want to work for Miniscule Industries. I think I'd be perfect for the job."

If you don't hear from the company in another few days, call to ask how long the job will be open. Don't be pushy, but make sure that your name keeps popping up when they think about possible candidates. If the job has gone to someone else, find out if there are any other jobs available. In addition, see if there was a specific reason they didn't hire you. You still might be able to convince them that you would be a good employee. It's never too late.

Be Positive

It may take a while to land a job. Don't let it get you down and don't take a rejection personally. Employers have a lot of different reasons for picking their employees, and if someone else gets the job you wanted, it isn't a reflection on your abilities. Your competition could have better connections or more experience. Or she might be able to work full-time, while you have to go back to school.

Melissa Courtright of Horsehead, New York worked one summer as a waitress for Ponderosa: "I went and filled out an application and waited forever for them to call me back, and then I had an interview and they hired me on the spot. The boss asked a few questions like what I'd do in certain situations, if I was responsible, if I'd get to work on time, stuff like that. She discussed the wages and that was about it. I tried to get across that I was a good worker and that I was responsible." The job, although not full-time, took up much of her summer: "I worked probably thirty hours a week. I would come in early in the morning and help open the restaurant. I was the one who put together the dining room. I worked from 9 to 2 during most weekends; it varied. They paid me $2.90 an hour plus tips." Melissa worked to have money for Christmas and then later for college: "If I didn't work, I thought I'd just be home during the day. I thought that if I had the money, I could go to the mall or the movies, and I wouldn't have to ask my parents for money." If you want to get a job in a restaurant, Courtright advises that you "go to a family restaurant, not something that's very fancy, but something in the middle. It's a good way to make money because you get tips." She also says that you should keep a positive attitude: "Grin and bear it when the customers aren't nice to you. The end of the day is always almost there."

A List of Positive Qualities to Impress the Interviewer

Responsible	Problem-solving ability
Friendly	Leadership
Energetic	Dedicated
Enthusiastic	Patient
Hard-working	Detail oriented
Computer literate	Good grades
Skilled in math	Initiative
Common sense	Confident
Writing skills	Mature
Honest	Flexible
Team worker	

WHAT HAPPENS WHEN YOU GET THE JOB

Getting a job is the first step. The next step is to do well so that they keep you and maybe even give you a raise. Although the job may seem fairly easy, there are a number of things that you can do that will impress your boss. Here are a few:

Don't Be Late

You want to do whatever it takes to be on time, especially on the first day. Employers hate it when their employees come in late and will be less than impressed if you can't make it to work on time. If you know you'll be late, call and explain why.

Dress for the Job

Don't be slovenly. The employer will want to see that you've made some effort to look good for work. Make him proud that he hired you.

Treat the Boss with Respect

We're not saying that you should lick her boots, but a boss usually feels that because she's signing your paycheck, she should be treated with respect. Do your best, and you're much more likely to get a raise.

Don't Get Caught Goofing Off

If you have the urge to talk with a friend on the company phone, be very careful not to get caught. Bosses hate it when you do your own thing instead of working, and if it happens often, you will probably get the axe.

Get Off Your High Horse

Many people we talked to didn't take their jobs seriously. They figured that since they were going to college, working as a car-parker was beneath them. Get over it. Your job will be a lot more fun and rewarding if you do good work and take it seriously. Plus, you might need to use your boss as a reference someday.

Do a Great Job, and Let Your Boss Know It

It almost goes without saying, but the best way to impress your boss is to do the work well. Work hard and pay attention to detail. But it's not enough to do the job right, you have to make it known: "Um. . . like. . . when I was cleaning under the cash register, I found this hundred dollar bill. . . Do you think it belongs to somebody?" or, "Hey, that was the fifth customer in a row who made a special effort to thank me, saying I'd given good service. You have such a nice clientele here." These are subtle ways to let your boss know how well you're doing.

WORKING AT CAMP

Most day and sleep-away camps hire young people to help with the daily tasks of making summer great for their campers, but for the most part, the paying jobs go to college students. If you're lucky, you might land a counselor position at a day camp. They do hire high school students as counselors-in-training (CIT) and waiters, but both of these positions pay little if any money. Many camps even expect you to pay the standard fee to go to camp and work one of these jobs. In other words, don't expect to get rich from a summer job at a camp.

Why Work a Job That Pays No Money?

At first glance, working at a camp for free might not seem like such a great thing, but if you want to get the experience, a CIT job might be right for you. If you work at a day camp, you'll still be able to spend the summer with your friends, and you'll have weekends off. You might even get paid. If you work at a sleep-away camp, you'll get the advantages of being at camp plus a little more responsibility.

Besides, a CIT job can lead to a counselor position later on. To become a counselor, you need camp experience, but the only way to get experience is to work as a CIT. If you're willing or able to work for little money now, you can get a better job later on. You should look at a CIT job as an internship, a way to set yourself up for some sweet summer jobs in the future.

Your chances at succeeding as a camp counselor are better if you have a specific talent. For example, if you can teach kids how to swim or play baseball or horseback ride, you'll find it easier to get a counselor job later on.

Joanna Riesman, of Montreal, Canada went to the same camp for years and ended up working there first as a CIT and then as a counselor: "I think it's great. You don't get paid very much, and if you haven't been at the camp, it might be difficult to enter the social scene. But if you do become a counselor, there are probably few situations that provide as much camaraderie and fun."

She remembers the time she ran an event called Color War: "My friends and I ran Color War, a three-day blast at the end of summer. As part of the event, we invented a complex water sports game involving every canoe, sailboat, and surfboard. At one point we looked out on the lake, and we realized that everyone was doing what they were doing because we had told them to. It was fun—exhilarating and ridiculous."

Although she loved the experience, she doesn't think it's for everyone: "If you like what camp is about, like canoeing, horseback riding, and playing tennis, you get to do these things with a little added responsibility. You don't get a lot of free time, but that's okay; your job feels like a vacation. There isn't a lot of privacy at most

camps, so you should do it only if you're the social type. You don't have to be athletic, but you have to like to do sporty things."

If you do decide to be a camp counselor, Riesman advises that you "bring lots of snack foods because the food is usually terrible. Bring more stuff than you think you need. I always just brought what they told us to bring. All the other kids brought other things, and they seemed to have a better time."

GOVERNMENT JOB PROGRAMS

You've probably seen it on TV or read it in the newspaper: the government wants to keep teenagers off the streets and put them to work. "Great," you think, "I'm a teenager, and I want to work. I'll apply." The jobs pay minimum wage, offer you valuable on-the-job training, and give you skills and experience to put on your college applications.

If you think you qualify for one of these jobs (there is an income requirement), call up the number before summer starts, and ask for info on how to get hooked up. We've included a list of phone numbers on page 34 for twenty large cities in America. You should know that getting answers from the government is not easy, and once you do get all the necessary information, you'll have to fill out a bunch of forms. Be persistent and don't get discouraged; these jobs can be a great way to get experience and are impressive references for colleges later on.

 Adina Dees of New York City, now a senior, has been incredibly successful getting summer jobs over her four years of high school. In tenth grade, Dees got a job at Harlem Hospital through the city's job program.

"They pick a few teenagers from 14 to 18 years old, and somehow through the luck of a lottery I got the job. I only got minimum wage, and I only worked four days a week. I had a lot of fun doing the job. I'm interested in biology and medicine. I made friends with the doctors, and they showed me stuff. I made the best of it; I mean, hey, a lot of people were like, 'I don't want to be here. I hate this job. I'm only making $4.25, and I could be making more somewhere else.' I looked at it like it was a learning experience.

"My job was to make appointments for cardiograms. When I started talking to the doctors about what they were doing, they took me into the rooms where they do surgery. The doctors were very friendly and were impressed that I was interested."

In eleventh and twelfth grade, Dees moved into the corporate world: "I was with this program called Prep for Prep that put some public school students in private high schools. As part of the program, they had a summer jobs bank sponsored by the corporations who had donated money to the program. They set up summer jobs for the students. I did data entry and learned some computer programs. The jobs paid well. Working in the corporate world is really weird. There's a corporate laugh that everyone has. I can't imitate it, but everyone did it."

Dee's skill at landing good jobs is partly due to her ability to present herself. She also follows some basic job-finding rules: "Getting a good job is all about networking and getting to know people. Get applications from anybody and everybody, and interview whenever you can. It all becomes easier as you keep doing it more and more. You have to know what these people are looking for, and know some background on the company. You should at least know what you're applying for. Also, dress in a way that is appropriate. If you go to the Gap, dress in casual clothes. If you go to the corporate world, wear a suit."

The Small Print

- *You must be between 14-21.*

- *Jobs are during the summer vacation from school.*

- *Job placement is in city, state, federal and nonprofit organizations only.*

- *The purpose is on-the-job training.*

- *You make minimum wage and higher depending on the city.*

- *The requirements to get a job are a social security number, citizenship or documentation that you have the right to work, and proof of family size and income level.*

Twenty Large Cities in the U.S. and their Department of Employment Phone Numbers

Baltimore, MD	(410) 396-1790
Boston, MA	(617) 727-6560
Chicago, IL	(312) 744-8379
Columbus, OH	(614) 645-7667
Dallas, TX	(214) 670-5908
Detroit, MI	(313) 876-0559
Houston, TX	(713) 658-3798
Indianapolis, IN	(317) 232-3101
Jacksonville, FL	(904) 630-1111
Los Angeles, CA	(213) 485-4675
Memphis, TN	(901) 576-6509
Milwaukee, WI	(414) 286-3751
New York, NY	(718) 488-1800
Philadelphia, PA	(215) 686-2359
Phoenix, AZ	(602) 262-4680
San Antonio, TX	(210) 207-7280
San Diego, CA	(619) 686-1920
San Francisco, CA	(415) 557-4800
San Jose, CA	(408) 277-4205
Washington, D.C.	(202) 724-7000

INTERNSHIPS

An internship is a paid or unpaid trainee position in which you learn the ropes of a certain job. As the economy changes and employers seek experienced workers, more and more people are gaining experience through internships. Because they give you experience with a good company, internships are one of the best ways to get started in a career. If you know that you're interested in a particular area, you might consider inquiring about an internship with a local company.

Even though most internships pay little or nothing, the competition for jobs among college students and recent grads is pretty intense. These people are looking for a career, and they know that one of the best ways to find one is by interning with a company that might hire them later on. You, as a high school student, will probably have to compete with people who have more education and more experience, so be ready to work for free over the summer.

How to Do It

Although we know of several great companies that set up internships for high school students (we list them on pages 37–38), let's assume that you want to work in your own area. You have to figure out in which field you want to intern. Are there any subjects in school that you like? Do you want to be a journalist or a television reporter? Are you into science or social work? Try to pick a career that might interest you, and then start the process of looking for jobs.

Start Early

The first thing you need to do is get an early start. If it's April, it's probably too late for this year unless you're incredibly lucky or have great connections. It takes a while to get an internship lined up, and the more advanced planning you do the better.

Use Connections

Just like finding a job (see the section on pages 15-21), finding an internship is much easier using connections. And believe it or not, everyone has connections. A connection is someone who knows you and might be willing to help you. The most obvious connections are parents and teachers.

Let's say that you want to intern at a television station. Begin by making this known to anyone who will listen. Ask if they know anybody in TV, and if they do, try to get them to make an introduction. Talk to your teachers, classmates, parents, parents' friends, and even people you meet on the streets. You want everyone you know to be helping you find an internship.

Make it Known That You'll Work for Free

Make it clear that if you find an internship in the field of your choice you will work for free. What company would refuse a well-mannered, ambitious, and eager young person a chance to work for them, especially if it doesn't cost anything? Although you might get lucky and find a paying job in a field that interests you, you'll increase your chances if you offer to work for nothing. Once a company sees how valuable you are, they may hire you the next summer and pay you some cash.

Check the Yellow Pages

Call up any business that is within your area of interest, and ask if they need people. Make it clear that you're a talented, intelligent young person who wants to learn from them, and tell them that you'll even work for nothing just to get some experience in the field. Just like when applying for paying jobs, be as professional as possible. Tell Ms. ____ how much you liked talking with her and then send her a note later in the week to remind her of your talk.

Try to Seem Older

Don't lie about your age, but make an effort to show how mature you are. Most people will happily hire a young intern who can help their company if they believe that the person is mature and willing to learn. Make the company feel that you will be a good worker.

Make the Most of the Experience

If you do get an internship, try your best to get something out of the experience. Many companies tend to give their interns busywork, like copying, stocking shelves, and stuff like that. Make it clear that you want to learn the harder tasks and try to make suggestions whenever you can. If you can get some real responsibility, you will get much more out of the experience and be able to use your skills later on.

A List of Great Internships

The following is a list of great internships that accept high school students [Source: *The Princeton Review Guide to America's Top 100 Internships*]. These companies do not provide housing, so contact a company only if you know you can find a place to stay in the area.

American Heart Association

Wallingford, CT   *(800) AHA-USA1*

St. Petersburg, FL

Omaha, NE

North Brunswick, NJ

Seattle, WA

Association of Trial Lawyers of America

Washington, D.C.   *(800) 424-2725*

Center for Investigative Reporting

San Francisco, CA   *(415) 543-1200*

The Feminist Majority

Los Angeles, CA   *(213) 651-0495*

Arlington, VA   *(703) 522-2214*

Forty Acres and a Mule Filmworks

Brooklyn, NY   *(718) 624-3703*

Inroads *(for minority students only)*

In 43 cities   *(314) 241-7330*

Marvel Comics

New York City, NY   *(212) 696-0808*

MTV: Music Television

New York City, NY   *(212) 258-8000*

National Aeronautics and Space Administration

Washington, D.C.	(202) 358-0000
Moffett Field, CA	(415) 604-5802
Greenbelt, MD	(301) 286-9690
Pasadena, CA	(818) 354-8251
Houston, TX	(713) 483-4724
Kennedy Space Center, FL	(407) 867-2512
Hampton, VA	(804) 864-4000
Cleveland, OH	(216) 433-2957
Marshall Airforce Base, AL	(205) 544-0997
Stennis Space Center, MS	(601) 688-3830

National Institutes of Health

Bethesda, MD	(301) 402-2176

Smithsonian Institution

Washington, D.C.	(202) 357-3102

Summerbridge National

20 locations nationwide	(415) 749-2037

Surfrider Foundation

San Clemente, CA	(800) 743-SURF

United Nations Association of the United States of America

New York City, NY	(212) 679-3232

Weyerhaeuser

Tacoma, WA	(206) 924-4403

VOLUNTEER WORK

One of the best things you can do this summer is help your community. Even if you have a job, you'll most likely have some free time to volunteer. Most charities are perfectly willing to work around your schedule. They need your help.

Here's How

To find a place to volunteer, look for an organization in your community that you'd like to help. Or, if you and your family belong to a church or synagogue, see if they can help you find something. Or maybe you know someone who works at a hospital that takes volunteers. By sticking with an organization that you already belong to or know about, you'll be sure to find out the details before you start working.

If you don't have any family or personal connections, check out the list of non-profit organizations that accept volunteers on pages 40-41. Identify yourself as a high school student and say that you're looking for ways in which you can help. They'll find work for you before you know it.

Robert Tichio of Paramus, New Jersey set up a Habitat for Humanity chapter in his high school. Habitat builds houses for the homeless and operates almost entirely with volunteers who raise money for supplies. They believe that the people who will live in the houses should help to build them as well. A campus chapter is an official organization that carries out the mission of Habitat by raising money, building homes, and educating the community.

Tichio got started because he wanted to do volunteer work: "The reason that I started with Habitat was that, like other high school students, I felt that it was important to have real-life experiences. While I think getting a job is important, I definitely think that volunteer experience can be a great idea for your summer." He also feels that there's no reason that you can't do both: "The most important key for any high school student is time management. It's important to be able to balance your time and manage your schedule. I worked at Barnes and Noble bookstore during the late shift from 4 to 11. I volunteered at Habitat from 8 to 3. I didn't work at both everyday, but being able to do both allowed me to earn money and help people at the same time."

Volunteering and starting the chapter at the same time did take its toll: "I didn't have free time. I was motivated and determined. I felt like I had to catch every brass ring. It was exhausting, but if I had to over again, I would do it just how I did it." But on the other hand, you don't have to volunteer as many hours as Tichio did: "There are people who are involved one day a week or one day a month. Anytime they want to participate is time well-spent. You don't have to contribute all your time. Naturally the more you participate the more you get out of it."

Getting the chapter started required a huge amount of work. Tichio began by researching volunteer organizations. He settled on Habitat because he liked their goals. Once he got the information, he began telling his classmates and principal

about it. "I wanted to share what I had learned with my school community. I informed them of what Habitat does. I wanted to make Habitat a part of my school."

Things were going smoothly until he found out about a New Jersey law that made it illegal for teenagers to use power tools. He was frustrated for a while, but the law changed and it was possible for the chapter to begin. Tichio had many experiences with bureaucracy and the legal system. "We had to rewire ourselves around the system. We were the first campus chapter in the state of New Jersey. Now that we had this opportunity, I said, 'Why don't we change this.'" What he learned about bureaucracy and policy will undoubtedly be valuable later on.

If you do decide to volunteer, Tichio advises that you, "believe in what you're doing. Volunteering doesn't give you any financial payment. The only thing you get is your satisfaction in doing something good. You have to be passionate in what you're doing and really believe in it. That's the only way you can get other people to believe it too. The founder of Habitat for Humanity said, 'The future of this movement lies with young people.' I'm positive that concerned students not only ensure a great future for this organization, but we also will become involved in shaping the future today."

The following is a list of nonprofit organizations that accept teenagers as volunteers. If you're interested in helping out our planet and the people who inhabit it, give one of these organizations a call.

Forty Nonprofit Organizations that Accept Teenage Volunteers

1. American Cancer Society — (800) ACS-2345
2. Easter Seals Society — (312) 726-6200
3. Salvation Army — (201) 239-0606
4. Historical Society — Check your phone book for a local historical society.
5. Ronald McDonald House — (708) 575-3571
6. Battered Women Shelters — Check your phone book for a local battered women shelter.
7. Boy Scouts of America, Inc. — (214) 580-2000
8. Save the Children Federation — (203) 226-7271
9. Association for Retarded Citizens — (817) 261-6003
10. American Lung Association — (212) 315-8700
11. Arthritis Foundation — (404) 872-7100
12. Planned Parenthood — Check your phone book for a local Planned Parenthood.

13. *Food for the Hungry*   (800) 2-HUNGER

14. *Mothers Against Drunk Driving*   (800) GET-MADD

15. *American Heart Association*   (214) 373-6300

16. *American Foundation for the Blind*   (212) 502-7600

17. *Volunteers for Peace*   (802) 259-2759

18. *United Way*   (703) 836-7100

19. *AIDS National Interface Network*   (202) 546-0807

20. *Alcoholics Anonymous World Services* (212) 870-3400

21. *Special Olympics*   (202) 628-3630

22. *The Cystic Fibrosis Foundation*   (800) 523-2357

23. *Soup Kitchens*   *Check your phone book for a local soup kitchen.*

24. *Make-a-Wish Foundation of America* (800) 722-9474

25. *March of Dimes*   (914) 428-7100

26. *The Humane Society of the United States*   (202) 452-1100

27. *National Multiple Sclerosis Society*   (212) 986-3240

28. *Coalition for the Homeless*   (202) 347-8870

29. *Rape Crisis Centers*   *Check your phone book for a local rape crisis center.*

30. *American Red Cross*   (202) 737-8300

31. *Audubon Society*   (212) 979-3000

32. *Big Brothers/Big Sisters*   (215) 567-7000

33. *Muscular Dystrophy Association*   (520) 529-2000

34. *American Diabetes Association*   (800) 232-3472

35. *Boys and Girls Club*   (404) 815-5700

36. *Habitat for Humanity*   (912) 924-6935

37. *Literacy Volunteers of America, Inc.*   (315) 445-8000

38. *Toys for Tots*   (202) 433-3612

39. *National Student Campaign Against Hunger*   (617) 292-4823

40. *National Wildlife Federation*   (202) 797-6800

STARTING YOUR OWN BUSINESS

Of course, a regular job or an internship might not be the way to go. There are other ways to make money. Why not try to start your own business?

Be an Entrepreneur

Although you might think that starting your own business would be difficult, it really isn't that hard to do. You just have to find out where there's a need and offer your services. Because you don't have to make a living from this job, you'll be able to offer competitive rates that are a good deal for you and the client. We're going to lay down the basics so that you can get started.

Offer a Service

The first step is to figure out what you want to do or sell. You want to find something that you can do that's valuable enough so that you'll actually make some cash. First, look for a need. Let's say you decide to cut lawns to make money ('cause most adults really hate cutting their grass). There are companies out there that take care of people's yards, but they're usually expensive. You can most likely offer the same service at a reduced rate. This might be a good opportunity.

Check Out the Competition

Once you've decided what you want to do, check to see what the competition is doing. If you decided to cut lawns, call up a few lawn services and see how much they charge. Ask them what services they provide, and find out what makes each company special. If they have any neat ideas—"We wash your windows too"—borrow them. Once you have their prices, find out if you can do the job for less.

Let the Market Set Your Prices

The easiest way to set your prices is to charge two-thirds of the competition's. Even though you'll be offering the same service, you won't be able to charge the same rate as your competitors when you first start. You won't have experience or an ad in the yellow pages, but you will still find people happy to hire you to save some money.

Make Sure it's Worth It

Calculate how much time it will take you to do the job, and how much you'll get paid. Work out an hourly rate. If you can cut a lawn in two hours, but you're only going to make is five bucks a lawn, you might consider another job. Try to set it up so that you'll be at least making more than minimum wage.

Don't forget to calculate the cost of equipment. If you're going to have to buy a lawn mower, you'll have to include that in your calculation. If it doesn't seem like you'll make enough money, don't do the job. Look for something else. Chances are, though, you'll find that you can offer a competitive rate and still make good money, because the competition will have a lot of expenses that you don't. They have to pay for office space, insurance, employee benefits, etc. Since you won't have to pay for these things, you'll be able to offer a good rate, and give your customers a good deal.

If you do a good job for a fair deal, you'll have customers lined up waiting for your services. Everybody appreciates a good deal, and the word will spread fast.

Let's say you find out that the competition charges $120 a month to cut lawns. You figure that if you were to be competitive, you could charge $80.

If the competition cuts lawns once a week, and you think it will take about two hours to cut a lawn, you'll be working approximately eight hours for $80, or $10 an hour.

But what if you have to pay for repairs on the mower? If you figure it will need $100 a season in repairs, you'll have to factor that into your cost. The more lawns you cut, the better the deal is.

If you have to pay for the lawn mower, then the whole situation gets a bit more complicated. A lawn mower would be what they call a capital expense. Because it will still have value after you get done using it, you'd have to figure out the amount that the value goes down over time. Let's say that the price of a used lawn mower is $200, and you think that at the end of the season you can sell it for $100. That means the lawn mower will cost you $100.

Advertise

Once you've decided on a service and set a price, you have to let people know that you're in business. The best way to do this is to advertise. You can put flyers in the post office, in the Laundromat, on car windshields, in lobbies, and in mailboxes, or you can call people you know. Once you get started you may get more work through word of mouth. A client might tell a friend of your great service, and you'll start getting phone calls.

Do a Good Job

Maybe this goes without saying, but if you don't do good work, you'll be out of business before you get started. If you make sure you're doing the best job you can, you'll get more work than you can deal with. Besides, it'll be more satisfying to do the job right.

 Chris Kensler of Evansville, Indiana worked at his own business the summer before his junior year. He helped businesses take inventory of their possessions: "I was working as a clerk for a law firm, a gopher. They had me do an inventory of their law firm. I just went around with a 35 millimeter camera and took a picture of everything. I took a picture of the building, the furniture, even the toilet for insurance purposes. I gave it to the office

manager who put values on each item, and then I did a computer printout that was coded to go with the pictures. We put the file in a fireproof safe so that if the building burned down they could get the insurance money.

"One of the partners at the law firm knew someone at a country club. I did all the same things for all their possessions, and then I sent a letter to the four other country clubs in Evansville. A couple of them said, 'lets do it.' By the end of the summer, I did three country clubs and the law firm. It was a great deal; I made two or three grand plus expenses."

Kensler is convinced that he had a huge advantage as a high school student. He could work cheaply, because the going rate for such a job was high: "No one had ever heard of it. Once they knew that such a thing existed, they were into it. Any price that I gave them was big for me, but for them it was nothing to guarantee a fair insurance payment in case of fire. To make money at your own business, find a niche and mine it."

SOME POSSIBLE ENTREPRENEURIAL IDEAS

Baby-sitting

Baby-sitting is the classic job for teenagers. It can sometimes pay well, and taking care of kids can be fun. There are a few things to be careful of, however. Certain kids are easier to sit for than others. Try to find out if anyone you know has sat for the people who are offering you a job. That way, you can get firsthand knowledge of how good (or bad) the kids really are.

If you want to make more money baby-sitting, consider setting up a special night in which you offer to take care of more than one family's kids. You could advertise that on every Friday night, you'll take care of neighborhood children for $4.00 a person per hour. This way, you'll be offering competitive rates, but at the same time, if you get five kids, you could make $20 an hour. Don't take on more than you can handle, though. It sounds easy when you're calculating how much you're going to make, but remember, these are kids that people have entrusted to your care. When children are small they tend to be very curious and get into everything, so they require a lot of attention. You'll also need to ask your parents if you can set aside a room in your home to operate your business out of.

The trick to setting up something like this is to be consistent. If you say you'll offer the service on Fridays, you have to be open every Friday. Maybe you can get a partner who's willing to cover for you on nights you can't make it. Also, you may have too many children one week. If that happens, you need to be able to get help.

There are a few things you can do to sell yourself as a baby-sitter. Many schools and libraries offer special first aid courses. If you can say that you've had this training, nervous parents will see that you're responsible enough to take care of their kids. In addition, you might want to have references ready. Keep a sheet with

Sample Calculation

To calculate whether a job will be profitable, look at every possible expense you can think of, and then calculate how much you'd have to work to pay off those expenses. In the example, this is what would happen if you cut 10 lawns a month:

Sample Expenses

Lawn mower repair and gas	$150
Lawn mower loss of value	($100 per season, $50 per month) $50
Fertilizer and grass seed	$30
Flyers to advertise	$10
Total Expenses	**$290**

Income

10 lawns @ $80 per household per month	$800
4 glasses of iced tea from that nice woman at 150 Oak St.	40¢
Total Income	**$800.40**

Net (Income − Expenses) $510.40

Hours (10 lawns, 4 times at 2 hours per lawn)	80 hours
Hourly Rate ($510.40 ÷ 80)	$6.38 an hour

phone numbers and names of happy customers so someone can check you out if they want.

Washing and "Detailing" Cars

You may already have experience in this, but it's a great way to make money. Washing cars, like cutting the lawn, is one of those jobs that adults hate. If you could offer to do it at a reasonable rate, you will have no shortage of customers. And if you offer to do a thorough cleaning of the inside of the car (detailing), you can charge even more money.

To start it up, you can set up a sign on the side of the road or advertise by putting flyers in people's mailboxes or (better yet) on car windshields. You may want to draw a small map on the flyers, directing possible customers to your place of business. Make it clear that you'll wash cars inside and out, and that you will leave the car looking great. Check out the prices local car washes charge and keep yours lower to bring people in.

House Cleaning

Another chore that people dread doing themselves is cleaning their house. After all, when you only have two days off a week, the last thing you want to do is spend one of them scrubbing the bathroom. You can easily get ten to twenty dollars an hour for this work. Call some different cleaning services to get an idea of what the businesses in your area are charging.

It might be a good idea to start with people who know and trust you, because you might be doing the work without anyone around. Keep in mind your client's privacy. Don't let them catch you reading stray pieces of mail or checking out their wardrobe. Another thing to think about is that this isn't the kind of cleaning you might do at home. You have to be *really* thorough. You've got to get all those crazy spots that you might not realize existed before now. There's no need for role reversal ("If I were a dust ball, where would I be?"), but a little extra effort could earn you a good reputation.

Summer Programs
and Activities

THE DIRT ON CAMP

Do the words *summer camp* bring to mind pictures of potholder weaving, bad movies about a guy running around in a hockey mask with an axe, and rounds of "Kumbaya" being sung until you want to throw up? It's an understandable conclusion—you probably had to endure such "fun" when you were a kid and your parents shipped you off for a few weeks each summer to sleep-away or day camp. They still might be into getting you off your butt and out there doing something, but now you've got a little more to say about what you want to do with your time.

Do you think you want to go into politics? Try a leadership camp. Do you want to explore the backwoods of Alaska? Try a wilderness camp. Do you want to go to Japan and live with a family? Try a homestay. There are camps for just about anything you can think of, from intense outdoor activity to focused creativity—and there's no basket weaving required.

Although there are some programs that are inexpensive, most charge a pretty big fee. So the first thing you have to decide (with a parent, no doubt) is how much money you're willing to spend. For the most part, the longer the program is, the more it costs. So once you decide how much you can spend, you can decide how long you can go.

From what we've heard from the interviews with people who have gone on these programs, most are well worth the money. You pay one price that includes everything—food, lodging, trips—and you get to experience things that you may never get to experience again. Some of the academically oriented programs allow you to get a head start in college, and many even offer classes that are more interesting than most first-year college classes. A trip could send you somewhere that you might otherwise never get a chance again to see. You'll meet interesting people *and* learn a lot.

YOUR OPTIONS

Here are some of the basic types of programs available.

Traditional Camps

These are camps set in scenic locations that teach you how to do outdoorsy things. Although many of these are for kids, some have programs for teenagers as well. In addition, you can go to these and be a CIT, which will give you some job experience.

Specialty Camps

There are a huge assortment of camps designed for people who want to specialize in different areas. If you have a good idea of what you want to do this summer, these might be for you.

Travel Programs

Itching to roam around the Painted Desert, see the Louvre, put a prayer in the wailing wall? If so, then these programs might be for you. They range from tours where everything is planned to homestays in foreign countries. Certain community service programs let you see the world and help people at the same time. And there are language programs that let you learn Spanish in Mexico or Chinese in Hong Kong. Whatever program you pick, you'll find that you can learn a great deal and have an amazing experience.

LESS-EXPENSIVE OPTIONS

As you check through this book, you'll find that a lot of these programs are expensive. The going rate for most of the programs is in the $3,000 to $4,000 range. We realize that these prices are too high for many of you, so here are some suggestions if you're on a budget.

Go Local

The least expensive summer option is day camp. Many communities will have summer programs that plan local activities so that you can return home at night. Because the camps don't pay for your room and board, they are much cheaper. On average, the going rate is about half of what the sleep-away programs ask, and many of these local programs are a lot of fun. Check out the day camps sections on pages 59 and 60 for information on how to find a good program.

The Ys Have It

There are some pretty great organizations out there that provide low-cost opportunities for the summer. Check out your local YMCA, YWCA, or YMHA. These organizations often run fun, affordable summer programs. Another good place to look is the local Jewish Community Center. Many JCCs have made it their mission to provide inexpensive trips and day camps over the summer. These camps are well run, and you don't have to be Jewish to go.

Jason Stork of New York, New York attended The 92nd Street Y's Camp 92, a teen day camp, the summer before his sophomore year. "It was a very fun time in my life. It had a big impact on me. I made friends for life. I'm still to this day, friends with people I met at camp. We'd do different activities around the city. They'd take us to dance clubs, comedy clubs, and theaters—all kinds of different things. They'd talk to us about being a teenager in the city, about AIDS, gender issues, and other stuff."

He especially remembers a day spent at a nearby Indian Reservation: "There was a particular day when the camp was split in half: male and female. We were taken to an Indian reservation. There we learned about life as a male and life as a female. We learned a lot about Indian culture and how they used to live. They taught us about how men took care of the family, and that we should be civil to each other. It got really deep."

One of the advantages of a Y camp is that the campers can be from many different cultures: "The camp was culturally and socially diverse. We learned about other people and their ways of life. There was one incident where we learned about racism. We had these scavenger hunts where we went through the city trying to find different things. We were sent into different communities throughout the cities. Pretty much every group that went out ran into some type of problem. Some stores wouldn't let you in. Name-calling started. It was a big learning experience for all of us, seeing neighborhoods we wouldn't normally have seen."

If you do go on a Y program, Stork advises that you "keep an open mind and heart to life. The experience is great. The Y has been a big influence on my life. People think it's all educational, but it's fun too. You learn how to deal with other people of different cultures and experiences."

Need-Based Scholarship Opportunities

Some local programs use a sliding scale to figure out the fees. If you can demonstrate need, you will pay less. In addition, many of the programs featured in the book have made it clear that they will offer substantial scholarships to high school students on the basis of need. These programs have the resources to provide help to a large number of students.

If you are looking for this type of help, you *must* apply early. Here is a list of programs that offer need-based scholarships:

> ***Adventure/Wilderness:***
> Outward Bound (page 70)
>
> ***Prep School Summer Programs:***
> Philips Academy at Andover (pages 132-133)
> Choate Rosemary Hall (pages 133-134)
> Northfield Mount Hermon Summer School (pages 137-138)
>
> ***On-Campus Programs:***
> Explorations at Wellesley (pages 146-147) (For inner-city Boston youth)
> Penn State University (pages 147-148)

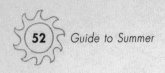

Travel Programs:
   American Field Service (pages 179-180) (For underserved minority groups)
   The Experiment in International Living (pages 181-182)
   Visions (pages 200-201)

Set Up Your Own Scholarship

If you don't have enough money to go on a program, you may be able to get money from somewhere else in the community. Because these programs are respected by so many people, you can often convince companies or organizations to help you pay your way. Here's how:

Pick a Worthwhile Program

You'll have more luck getting financial help from others if you pick a program that is educational or is related to community service. Any of the community service programs, the homestay programs, and the prep school programs are good candidates for getting financial aid. Two excellent programs for which you can raise money are Earthwatch's scientific expeditions and Interlocken's community service programs. Both of these programs are tax-deductible, so a contribution to your cause costs very little money.

Look for Local Help

If you know of any local community organizations, check out their scholarship programs. You might find that they are affiliated with some of the programs that we've listed. Look for local organizations like Kiwanas, Lion's club, Mason's Service, Junior League, and the Optimist Club. These organizations might be convinced that you are a worthwhile cause and may contribute some money.

Also look for business organizations and check out the local chamber of commerce. If you can prove that the program you want to attend is worthwhile, you might be able to convince them to help you with the funding. Check out your relatives' employers. Also, ask your guidance counselors and your teachers if there are some established scholarships in your area.

Don't Give Up

Although the price for some of the programs listed may seem prohibitively expensive, it is possible to raise the funds. Pick one that is either inexpensive or that offers scholarships so that you need to raise less money, and then start fundraising as soon as possible. You might not be able to go this coming summer but stick with it to save up for the next summer.

 During her sophomore year in high school, Molly Carleton from Chippenhook, Vermont raised the money to attend the Experiment in International Living's program in France: "Because my mom had been on an Experiment program in college, she got this mailing. I didn't know

that they had a program for kids my age, so when I found out, I got all excited and I wrote for more information. It was really amazing that kids my age could to do this stuff. You can't go by yourself to Europe when you're sixteen. The program requires a passport, so I had to get the passport, and then send a $275 deposit from my own money that I had been saving from baby-sitting and working at a bakery."

"I got a money order, and my mom was freaking. My parents weren't mad or anything, but financially they couldn't help me at all. They didn't think I'd be able to go. So I sent the application and got accepted, but there was still the scholarship stuff to worry about. There was all this awful waiting."

The Experiment's financial aid department got Molly a $2,000 scholarship from Reader's Digest. "The requirement was that I had to write a little paper about my experiences. Even with their help I wasn't going to have enough of my own money. It was a total of $3,400 for the trip. I found some local help through the guidance counselor at school. They gave me $900. The rest I came up with myself from working. I got $100 from my grandmother and $50 from two of my aunts. I just saved everything I had."

"It was really worth it. It was a lot of paper work and saving and depriving myself of movies and other stuff, but I don't think I'll have an opportunity to do this type of thing again. Later on, I'll have college and other stuff to worry about. It's something you have to do when you have the opportunity."

In the end, her parents were impressed with their daughter's initiative: "I didn't get that much support in the beginning, but my parents were really proud in the end. It was my first airplane ride and my first time out of the country. It was a great experience."

CAMP ADVISORY SERVICES

If you do choose to go to a camp or a summer program, you'll want to make the decision carefully. The problem, however, is that there are so many programs to choose from. How are you going to find which one is right for you?

Experts can help. Because of the huge range of choices involved, camp advisory services have cropped up. Student Camp and Trip Advisory, for example, sends two evaluators to every camp in the country. These people go to the wilderness camps, the foreign language camps, and community service camps around the world evaluating their quality. Also they get feedback from the people who have gone to camps on their recommendation.

To Each Her Own

Each summer program has its own personality. Advisors can help match you up with the right program. They also will help you eliminate camps with bad reputations.

This is the way it works. You meet with an advisor who tries to get a feel for what you like and dislike. Are you more comfortable by yourself or in big groups?

Are you competitive or not? Do you want to travel abroad? They try to figure out what you want to get out of a summer program and then suggest to you one that will be fulfilling.

Good advisors can get a sense of who you are and what you like. If you have special needs—dietary or physical, for example—they can find the perfect camp. Their services are invaluable, so if you know of a good one in your area, take advantage of it.

And the Best Part

Most of these services do not charge you a penny. They make their money from programs who pay a referral fee to the advisory service. This is a great thing, but something to think about. Some unscrupulous services might send you to programs that pay the highest fee. Make sure you check out the service that you use. Find out how much research they do, and how they come up with their recommendations. Below, we list the two national services that we wholeheartedly recommend. If you want to use one of these services, call its toll-free number for a location near you.

How to Judge a Camp Advisory Service

Although a few advisory services, like SCATA, are national, you may not live in an area where there is an office around. Because there's so much variability in the quality of these services, take some time to determine if the one you want to use is any good. Ask this pointed question: how do you get information about each camp? The advisory service should have something besides brochures for finding out about camps. Try to find out exactly how they go about it. A good advisory service will use information from the camps and their own research. Also, ask for the names of some people who have used the service. Ask these people if they felt the service was useful and if the recommended camp had been what they were looking for.

A good advisory service can make your life a lot easier and practically guarantee a good camp experience. It's a free way to get some great ideas.

Two Great Camp Advisory Services

Student Camp and Trip Advisory
161 Highland Ave., Suite 104
Needham, MA 02194
(800) 542-1233

Locations in Massachusetts, Rhode Island, Connecticut, Georgia, Florida, Michigan, Illinois, California, Montreal, and Brazil.

Student Summers
68 Harvey Drive
Short Hills, NJ 07078
(201) 467-2640

Locations in Short Hills, NJ, Rivervale, NJ, and Washington, D.C.

HIKING ON YOUR OWN

Although it might seem like an easy thing to do, hiking in the wilderness takes preparation. Many beginners make the mistake of just going to a wilderness area with a tent and walking aimlessly. Don't fool yourself; this really can be dangerous. Many people choose to start their wilderness experience with one of the summer programs listed on pages 62-73. If you're a little nervous, try one of these programs to show you the ropes, and then later on you can go with a few friends. On the other hand, given the right preparation, hiking with friends can be both safe and a blast.

Quality Time with Mom

No matter where you live in the United States, it's a short trip to Mother Nature. This summer might be the perfect time to start hiking, to get out of the city or the suburbs, and hang with Mom.

Here's the scoop. Start out with an easy trip. Don't try to climb Mount Everest on your first outing. To get a sense of what would be a good first trip, contact your local hiking club. They will have maps and loads of suggestions. It's also a good idea to bring an experienced hiker with you on your first trip. You'll get a lot more out of the experience.

Be Prepared

Before you go on any hike, make sure you know where you're going. Tell somebody where you're going and when you'll be back in case something happens. Let somebody know your exact route too, so she can find you. In national and state parks, you can give this information to the ranger on duty. As much as you value independence, don't take a chance.

Don't Go It Alone

Although you might think it cool to hike in the woods by yourself, it's extremely dangerous. What happens if, say, you twist your ankle, and you're miles away from any kind of help? Hiking is not like a day at the beach. Besides, it's a lot of fun to go with a few friends. You'll have people to talk with, and being outside in nature brings out the best in everyone.

These Boots Are Made for Walkin'

Your feet deserve decent, comfortable boots. There's nothing worse than having blisters on your feet when you have many miles to go. In addition, you should bring lots of water and food. Hiking takes a lot of energy, so it's good to have nourishment.

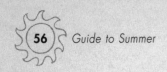

Check the Weather

Remember, if it rains or if a thunderstorm starts, you might be in trouble. Bring lightweight, packable rain gear (but, if at all possible, avoid rainy days). If the forecaster says rain, wait for a nicer day. Even if it's supposed to be sunny, bring rain gear anyway. The weather changes quickly in the mountains.

But It Was Such a Pretty Color

As much as you might want to eat that tasty-looking mushroom on the side of the trail, don't do it. Don't eat any plant unless you have the advice of a professional guide. You should use common sense in general. For example, don't stand too close to the edge of a cliff or start any fires. Bring food to eat that you don't need to cook.

The Road Less Traveled

If you are planning on hiking on your own or with a program you should check out the following books:

The Complete Walker, by Colin Fletcher. This book is a guide to the philosophy of hiking. Beautifully written, it will tell you both how and why to hike. If you can't find this particular book, anything by Fletcher is a good guide to the outdoors.

Backpacker's Handbook, by Chris Townsend. This book is a guide to the fundamentals of camping and will give you solid info.

Soft Paths, by Bruce Hampton and published by the National Outdoor Leadership School. This is a great guide to low-impact camping.

Annapurna, by Maurice Herzog. This is a great book about an outdoor adventure.

Desert Solitaire, by Edward Abbey. This is another book about surviving in the wilderness.

To find guidebooks for hiking, check out:

> *Adventurous Traveler Bookstore*
> *P.O. Box 577*
> *Hinesburg, VT 05461*
> *(800) 282-3963   (802) 482-3546*
> *email: books@atbook.com*

Also, you might want to look at *Backpacker Magazine*. It has great stories and advice for adventurers.

ORGANIZED SPORTS

Over the summer, you can find all kinds of sports leagues in your community. You can find leagues or programs in baseball, basketball, boxing, bowling, badminton, anything and everything. By joining one of these, you can enjoy playing sports without having to worry about keeping up with classes. Even if you've never played in a sport in high school, summer is the perfect time to try. In addition, there are special sports camps where you can concentrate on a specific activity (see pages 74-79).

But First . . . How Good Are You?

There are so many different ways to play sports. You can play pick-up games with your friends or you can join a league. The first thing that you should decide, however, is just how serious you are about the sport, because there's a chance to play in most sports at every level. If you've never played before and you're not too athletic, don't put yourself in a situation where everybody is trying to impress pro scouts and you spend most of the time picking splinters out of the bench. On the other hand, if you're confident in your skills, look for something competitive. You want to be challenged, so you should look for a situation in which you'll be either as good as everyone else or a tiny bit behind.

How to Find a Sports League in Your Area

You probably have an idea of how good you are. Maybe you play in school and are the star of the team or maybe you have trouble walking and talking at the same time. In either case, you can find the right situation. In addition to the specialty sports camps listed later in the book, there are a lot of local programs in just about every city. The first place to look is at your high school. Ask your gym coaches or your guidance counselor if they know of any leagues. See if your high school sponsors sports over the summer.

Next, try the local parks and recreation department. Many will know of leagues and some sponsor athletic events. Don't be afraid to participate just because you haven't tried before or you think you can't do it. There are leagues for every level of ability; just go for it.

The last place to check is at local sporting-goods stores. Ask them if they know of any leagues or places to play. Since many provide uniforms, they'll help you find a team.

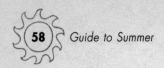

Individual Sports

If you plan to exercise on your own, set up a schedule for yourself. Figure out how many days a week you want to practice and stick to it. A lot of people start their summers with grand plans only to give them up at the end of a week. Consider yourself in training for the fall.

There's nothing quite like returning to school in great shape, looking like you've been outside all summer. While your friends sat around glued to the sofa, you were getting up every morning and running a few miles or rollerblading. If you don't already, you'll be amazed at how great you feel when you exercise regularly. Just pick something fun and stick to it.

TRADITIONAL CAMPS

Another way to enjoy being outdoors over the summer is to go to traditional summer camp. For generations, summer has been synonymous with camp for millions of kids.

S'mores No More

"But wait a minute," you might say, "camps are for kids." Some of you may have already gone to camp a few times. But now that you've grown out of those Grr-animal outfits, you may think that camps are no longer for you. This isn't true. There are plenty of camps that are geared toward teenagers, and there are plenty of camps that will give you an educational and exciting camp experience.

In the old days, a "camp" was a place in the country where you went to learn all kinds of outdoor activities and to give your parents some peace. Today, you have a bit more to choose from. First, there are wilderness camps, which take that roughing-it thing to a new extreme. In these programs, you'll learn how to hike and live in the wilderness. Then, there are specialty camps, which allow you to learn about one specific subject with a group of like-minded kids. There are music camps, computer camps, sports camps, and more.

Basically, there are two types of traditional camps: day and sleep-away camps. Both function exactly as their names indicate. A day camp is one from which you go home each night. A sleep-away camp has sleeping cabins for campers.

Day camps have a couple of advantages over sleep-away camps. First of all, they're significantly cheaper. They can offer you lower prices because the camps don't have to feed you breakfast, lunch, and dinner, or provide you with a place to stay. Secondly, you'll be at home. Although this might be a disadvantage to some who want to get away for a while, being at home allows you to continue seeing your friends.

On the other hand, if you do go to a sleep-away camp, you'll get to experience many things that you couldn't at home. You'll have opportunities to try things with the help of counselors. Since you spend much of your time in sleep-away camp with the same group of people, you're likely to become close. It can be a great place to meet people.

Day Camps

There are many day camps available. From sports camps to traditional day camps, you will find one that appeals to you. Since these camps are local, it is impossible to list them all, but we will help out with a guide to choosing one.

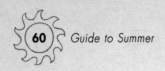

The Princeton Review Way of Choosing a Day Camp

First, check in the local newspaper and yellow pages for a list of camps. See if there are any that interest you. If you like sports, try a football or tennis camp. If you like chess, there may be a camp for you.

Second, call the camp and ask for references. Most camps will have a list of people and their phone numbers. Call these references and ask them questions about the camp, but don't just ask them if they had a good time. Instead, ask them more specific questions. "Did the camp live up to your expectations?" or "The advertisement claims that the food is cooked by four-star chefs . . . was it any good?" Try to figure out if the camp is what it's advertised to be. If the camp claims to be the "Michael Jordan Basketball Camp," see if his Airness was actually there.

After you get done asking these questions, find the name of another camper: "Could you give me the name of someone else who went to the camp?" And then ask that camper the same kind of questions. This way you can be sure that the first reference from the camp wasn't, say, the owner's daughter.

Finally, visit the camp. Get a sense of where you'll be spending your days. Maybe the camp is set away in a natural setting. Maybe it's in a rickety high school gym. Before you commit to going, make sure you know where you'll be.

Welcome to the Occupation

For many of you, day camps are better for finding jobs. Although many sleep-away camps won't hire high school students, day camps will sometimes hire seventeen- and eighteen-year-olds to work as counselors. Check out pages 31-32 for the inside scoop of working in camp.

Sleep-away Camp

Sleep-away camp is about being more independent and getting away from your parents. Because of this, the bonds that you make at camp may be stronger than many you make at school. Some of the people we interviewed spent years at the same summer camp and are still close to the people they met there even after ten years. Some are even married to people they met at camp.

In addition, going to a sleep-away camp can give you the opportunity to explore different areas of the country. You can see the Rockies in Colorado or the beauty of Maine. Some of the wilderness camps we list are located in several locations. You might white-water raft in one national park and then climb a mountain in another.

Old Habits Are Tough to Break

If you have been going to the same camp for years and you have a group of friends that you see there each year, by all means go back to that camp. Many friendships that develop over the summers will continue throughout your adult life.

On the other hand, if you're thinking of attending a camp that accepts people from elementary school on, and you have never attended before, you might want to think twice. A lot of times, the kids who come back year after year form cliques that are hard to break as a newcomer. It would be like going to a new high school. This isn't to say that it's too late to try out a new camp. Maybe decide to go to a camp with a friend or two so that you know you won't be by yourself if you're worried about that. Who knows? The other campers might all be sick of the usual crowd and happy to see a new face.

For the most part, camps that are set up for older campers have a more challenging set of activities than the ones for kids. Many camps have a special wilderness program that allows you to practice surviving in the wild. Many have some type of special feature that sets them apart from the rest of the camps. They may teach you to fly an airplane or to kayak down a raging river. You will most likely be challenged to do things you wouldn't normally do.

Counselors in Training and Waiters

Many traditional camps "hire" returning older campers as counselors-in-training (CITs) or waiters. These jobs can be a great way to get experience for a counselor job when you get to college. For more on this, see pages 31-32 in our jobs section.

TEEN CAMPS

The following is a listing of some of the best traditional summer camps that are designed for teenagers. We have tried to choose camps that are not only well-respected and fun to attend, but that will give you a chance as a newcomer.

Maine Teen Camp

Address (Winter) 180 Upper Gulph Rd., Radnor, PA 19087; (Summer) RR 1 Box 39 Kezar Falls, ME 04046

Phone (Winter) (800) 752-2267 (610) 527-6759 **Fax** (Winter) (610) 520-0182; (Summer) (207) (Summer) 625-8581 Fax (207) 625-8738

Costs $2,495-$4,195

Ages 13-17

Size of program 220 campers

Length of camp 28-42 days

Application deadline Early applications are preferred. They're processed in the order they're received.

Description A traditional camp for teens

Summary A great camp if you want to experience summer camp in an environment geared for high school students

History Since 1984, Maine Teen Camp has provided a beautiful setting for teenagers who want to enjoy a traditional camp experience, but Maine Teen Camp attempts to offer more than the traditional camp programs. It has

excellent sports, arts, and wilderness activities, and as they make abundantly clear in their brochure, there's no required swimming or competitions.

The Program At Maine Teen, you design your own program. Your first day is spent touring the facilities and meeting the leaders. Then you get to choose in which area you want to concentrate. Maine Teen's large variety of programs makes it easy to experiment in different areas, so you can try things that you might not be able to do in high school.

They have a ropes course, beautiful beaches, windsurfing, water-skiing, basketball, soccer, and mountain biking, just to name a few. Most of the programs are taught by experts in their fields. Basketball, for example, is taught by experienced college players.

In addition, they offer day trips, overnights, and longer trips. You might canoe down the nearby Saco river, or climb New Hampshire's Presidential Range. The camp is a great place to enjoy the great outdoors.

 Ayelet Amittay of Newton, Massachusetts went to Maine Teen Camp and was really impressed: "This was my first time at sleep-away camp. I was really mortified. I was not happy that I was going, but I had such a good time that I have to go back next year. The counselors were so wonderful, and they encouraged us to have fun. There was a group of kids there for everybody. I learned how to do so many things I never thought I'd be able to do. I got to water-ski for the first time. It was terrifying, but I tried it and it was quite an experience."

She was especially impressed with how easy the counselors made it to try new things: "It's just so much freedom and opportunity. It's a great place to go." She remembers when the counselors put on a skit based on the dating game: "One counselor dressed up as a nerd. Another woman counselor dressed as a man. It was the funniest thing I'd ever seen. It just shows how the counselors work really hard to have fun."

If you do go to Maine Teen Camp, Amittay advises that you "keep an open mind. Be willing to try new things, to meet different types of people. Try to be friendly with everyone, which is really easy because all the people are so great."

Med-O-Lark

Address 560 Harrison Ave., Suite 407, Boston, MA 02118

Phone (800) 292-7757 (617) 423-2200
Fax (617) 423-2065;
(Summer) (207) 845-2441

Costs $2695 or $4360

Ages 11-16

Size of program 200 campers

Length of camp 28-56 days

Application deadline Early applications are preferred. They're processed in the order they're received.

Description A traditional camp for young adults

Summary A good place for your first camp experience. A safe environment with great counselors.

History For the last twenty-four years, Med-O-Lark camp has been run by Neal Goldberg. The camp offers a safe and nurturing experience for teens who want a traditional camp.

The Program Med-O-Lark is a traditional camp that is reserved for teenagers. You'll be able to do all the things you might imagine. These include sailing, candle-making, jazzercise, tie-dye, Ultimate Frisbee, video production, water-skiing, windsurfing, pottery, a ropes course, sailing, guitar, etc. You'll get to take classes in different camp subjects, and you should finish the summer with a great experience outdoors.

Med-O-Lark makes an effort to make the transition to camp life easy for everyone, even the first-time camper. They do this by putting the experienced campers with newcomers. They also give special attention to first-time campers to help them get acclimated to camp life.

On a typical day, you'll spend the morning and afternoon in camp classes, and spend the evening doing a number of activities ranging from acting in plays to performing in magic shows. The director of the camp has years of experience presenting magic shows and will gladly pass on his knowledge.

 Sarah Werner went to Med-O-Lark when she was fifteen years old. It was her first camp experience, and she loved it: "It was the best experience of my life. It was incredible. Being able to meet new people from all over the world was really different. Everyone went there to meet new people and make new friends and do exciting things. I'm still in touch with the friends I made."

One of her favorite camp experiences was the arts festival given by the counselors at the end of the program. All the campers were taken away from camp, and the counselors set up the show. "When we came back, all the counselors had put up lights and had draped the arts and crafts room so it looked like a gallery. They had everyone's work displayed on velvet, and you got to see what everyone had done that month."

She lived with twelve other girls in a cabin: "We were the oldest group and we were CITs, so we had special privileges. They took us out of camp a lot, and we got to go do things with the guy CITs." Werner feels that to enjoy the camp, you have to keep a positive attitude: "The first day was hard. Most of the people had been there. The thing I told myself was to keep smiling, because if I was negative it would ruin my whole month. Just be positive and friendly because it gets better every day."

WILDERNESS CAMPS

If you really want to rough it, why not try one of the wilderness camps in the country? Certain camps are designed to give you the experience of living outdoors in the remaining wilds of the U.S. In some of these programs, you will be taught how to survive in the wilderness and then given a chance to make a solo trip. By learning these survival skills, you may even learn something about tackling the adventures of life.

There are wilderness programs for every level of experience. Even if you've never slept without the whir of traffic on a nearby interstate, you'll still be able to find a program for you. We have listed these programs in order of difficulty. The first programs are fairly laid back. You'll be able to take a shower almost every day, and you'll be camping in relative luxury. The last few programs are really challenging. You will learn how to survive on your own in the wild.

Longacre Expeditions

Address RD 3 Box 106, Newport, PA 17074

Phone (800) 433-055127 (717) 567-6790
Fax (717) 567-7853

Costs $1,495-$3,495

Ages 11-19 (participants for the more popular trips are grouped by age)

Size of group 10-18 participants with 2-4 counselors

Lengths of programs 15-41 days

Application deadline Early applications are preferred. They're processed in the order they're received.

Description Wilderness trips in Pennsylvania, New England, Colorado, Pacific Northwest, and Central America

Summary A good program for anyone looking for a wilderness trip, but especially good for beginners. Large enough to ensure that you will be grouped with people your own age.

History Longacre Expeditions, established in 1981, is a well-respected wilderness program that offers adventures for all different levels of

experience. The carefully planned trips will give you a chance to explore several facets of the wilderness experience within one fifteen-to-twenty-eight–day program.

A typical program Longacre's programs are like little trips in that you spend a few days at a bunch of different locations.

One of Longacre's more popular trips takes you to Blue Ridge in the wilds of Pennsylvania. On the first day of the program, you'll be swinging through the air on a 700 foot zip line and climbing a wall that's at least twice as tall as you are. Challenging though this may seem, you'll be supervised by expert staffers who will make sure that you come through with flying colors. By the end of the day, you'll hit your sleeping bag, dead tired, but by morning you'll be ready to wake up and face another day.

Over the course of the program, you'll travel by bike and foot to a large area of the Pennsylvania backcountry. Although you'll be carrying food and shelter on your back, you won't be totally roughing it. At many of the camp sites, you'll find bathrooms and showers, and your backpack won't be so heavy that you can't make it. Before the trip is done, you'll have gone white-water rafting, rock climbing, and biking around the back roads of Pennsylvania. The last few days of the program are spent exploring the caves of Reeds Gap State Park. By the time you get home, your group will be a skilled backpacking machine. Most people get done with the experience amazed at just how much they have learned and accomplished.

A program like this is a good chance to get your feet wet (sometimes literally), to learn what it's like to explore the great outdoors with only your wits and whatever you can carry on your back. At the same time, you'll have experts to make sure that the trip goes well. In addition, if you're ready for an advanced trip, Longacre has several of these available. They offer intermediate and advanced trips that can challenge the most physically fit adventurers.

 Lauren Pinkus of Philadelphia, Pennsylvania went on a Longacres sailing trip the summer before she entered ninth grade. The program, Can-Am Bike-Sail, began with the campers spending almost two weeks biking through miles of spectacular countryside and then sailing for two weeks at Maine's Wooden Boat School. There, they learned to sail under Coast Guard–certified instructors. According to Pinkus, who has since gone on more advanced outings, the trip was "cushy...we stayed at national campgrounds. There were showers and other facilities with campers staying in tents and trailers."

"At night the campers got together in a circle to thank the instructors. It definitely ties everything together. Towards the end of the session, you're telling them everything. It was great. It united everybody."

Even though the weather was horrible (it rained every day during the sailing part), it was still a great time. According to Pinkus, "We slept late, woke up, then we went sailing. After the day was over we'd play Ultimate Frisbee and hang out. It was really fun." Just like many other Longacre campers, Pinkus was hooked and can't wait to get out to the wilderness again. But such a trip isn't for everybody. "You have to be willing to get dirty," she said, "and you can't be scared of bugs."

Trailmark

Address 16 Schuyler Rd, Nyack, NY 10960

Phone (800) 229-0292; (914) 358-0262

Costs $1,295-$2,795

Ages 12-17 (participants for the more popular trips are grouped by age)

Size of group About eighteen participants with three counselors

Lengths of programs 15-28 days

Application deadline Early applications are preferred. They're processed in the order they're received.

Description Wilderness and horseback riding trips in New England, the Northwest, the Southwest, and the Rockies

Summary A good program for anyone looking for a wilderness trip but especially good for beginners. Offers some freedom within each trip. Large enough to ensure that you will be grouped with people your own age.

History Trailmark's founders, Rusty and Donna Pedersen, have been working in summer camping programs all of their lives, and they have succeeded in making Trailmark one of the best wilderness programs around.

Through a combination of carefully planned itineraries and well-trained guides, Trailmark is an excellent introduction to the rigors of wilderness camping.

The Program One of Trailmark's goals is to give its participants a few contrasting experiences within a small geographic area. So if you spend some time near the coast, you will later move to the mountains. Trailmark's most popular trip is its twenty-eight-day trip through New England. A combination of biking, mountain climbing, canoeing, white-water rafting, roping, and rock climbing, the New England trip will give you a sense of the possibilities of the outdoors. In this trip, you start by making your way through a Project Adventure ropes course, an obstacle course in the sky. Then you spend some time hiking around the coast of Maine.

After you get done with the hiking, you move to Acadia National Park where you split off into smaller groups. Some people will bike on a road, some will mountain bike, and some will just hike. You will climb Mt. Katahdin, Maine's highest mountain, and see a glorious view of thousands of acres of unspoiled wilderness. Then (after you catch your breath) you paddle a canoe down a river and, finally, the trip ends with white-water rafting.

Trailmark is a great program for your first time in the wilderness, but they do offer some more advanced programs as well. The counselors are well trained, and you will have experts instructing you in any of the more difficult tasks like rock climbing or white-water rafting.

 James Carifa of New Jersey went with Trailmark on their twenty-eight-day backpacking trip to the Southwest. He felt the trip was perfect for someone who wanted to learn about the wilderness but was not ready to go on his own. The program had many different aspects: hiking, a service project, mountain biking, and white-water rafting.

Carifa's favorite day was when he and his group decided to hike to a snow-covered mountain: "There was this one hike. We hiked up a mountain. And toward the top there was all this snow. We stopped and we were eating lunch. There was this one hill. We strapped on our rain suits and walked up there. And we started sliding down. It was so odd that it was summertime, and we could walk up a hill and there was snow."

Even though they were camping, the actual living conditions were not too rough: "We stayed in a campground usually. We basically lived out of a van. We had tents and stuff. We had three people to a tent. Everyone rotated so every week you were with two other people. Every few days we'd be going through a town and stop at a private campground and shower and do our laundry. It was comfortable."

Carifa's advice for someone going on a Trailmark program is to "be friends with everyone. Don't form a little clique with three other people. Try to be friendly with everyone in the group because you'll have more fun that way."

America's Adventure

Address 2245 Stonecrop Way, Golden CO 80401

Phone (800) 222 3595 (303) 526 0806
Fax (303) 526-0885

Costs $1,988-$3,888

Ages 12-17 (participants for the more popular trips are grouped by age)

Size of group Fewer than fifteen people per group

Lengths of programs 21-42 days

Application deadline Early applications are preferred. They're processed in the order they're received.

Description Wilderness, biking, horseback riding, and sailing trips in the Pacific Northwest, Canadian Rockies, Hawaii, and the Southwest

Summary A good but challenging program for anyone looking for a wilderness trip. Large enough to ensure that you will be grouped with people your own age.

History America's Adventure has been running adventure travel programs since 1976, and, although they do offer one easy trip (called Bold West), most of their programs are fairly challenging. They push you to try new things and to learn how to survive in the wild. These programs are not for the faint of heart. If you cannot imagine going to the bathroom in the woods, you should choose another program.

A typical program One of America's Adventures most popular trips—Boot, Saddle & Paddle—has many of the features that have made America's Adventures so successful. You start by getting on a horse and making your way through the mountains of Colorado. Just like in the old west, you'll be carrying your supplies on packhorses and mules that follow the convoy. If you've never ridden before, you'll be given an easy horse that won't cause you much trouble.

After the riding, you'll get on a raft and travel down the Colorado River through rapids. The views are amazing, and your instructors will teach you about the geological formations of this beautiful area. Then you'll hike into Havasu Canyon where you'll experience waterfalls and modern Native American culture. The last part of the trip is through different Indian reservations. America's Adventure makes you record everything you experience by asking you to keep a journal of your activities.

America's Adventure is a great program for those looking for a challenging adventure, but it might not be the best program for your first trip to the wilderness. America's Adventure is for those who are willing to take risks and push themselves to gain a great wilderness experience.

 David Goldman of Bethesda, Maryland went on America's Adventure Peak Five program, which has white-water rafting, rock climbing, backpacking, windsurfing, and mountain biking. The twenty-eight-day program was well planned: "All the instructors knew what they were doing," according to Goldman, who overcame his fear of heights by climbing in Rocky Mountain National Park. Rock-climbing is supervised, with one instructor leading two campers over the crags and cliffs of the park.

The program really pushed the participants: "The first day of hiking was really hard, I was like . . . I don't know about this," said Goldman, who found the entire trip exhilarating. But by the end of the trip he was an old hand who could hike with the best of them. Goldman's favorite part of the trip was the mountain biking. A van followed the bikes with spare parts and all the food that might be needed, and the participants had to work hard to explore the Grand Mesa of Colorado.

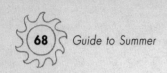

"The trip is not posh. It's a real outdoors experience. We only got to take two or three showers the whole month." said Goldman. He did point out, however, that the windsurfing segment in the middle of the trip was a welcome break from living out of a backpack. A trip with America's Adventure is a real adventure that will challenge you and teach you what it's like to live in the outdoors.

Interlocken—Crossroads Student Travel

Address Interlocken RR2 Box 165, Hillsboro, NH 03244

Phone (603) 478-3166
Fax (603) 478-5260

Costs $1,895-$2,995

Ages Finishing grades 7-12

Size of group 13 students with 2 leaders

Lengths of programs 21-28 days

Application deadline Early applications are preferred. They're processed in the order they're received.

Description Adventure/wilderness trips in California, the Southwest, New England and Colorado

Summary A challenging adventure program for those who don't need coddling

History Started in 1967 by Interlocken (an international summer camp), Crossroads Student Travel gives you a chance to engage in cross-cultural exploration and physical challenges. The wilderness trips will teach you what you need to live in the wilderness. They range from moderately challenging to very tough.

A typical program One of the more difficult Crossroads programs, the Western Wilderness program in Colorado, will give you an idea of how they structure their trips. You'll begin by meeting in Grand Junction where you'll spend a couple days outfitting the expedition, and planning the program. Because crossroads is teaching you how to do one of these on your own someday, you'll be involved in every stage of planning the trip.

Next, you go to Telluride where you'll learn how to rock climb. They'll teach you knots and rappelling (sliding down a rope), and although you'll be with skilled guides, the climbing will be scary. After learning how to handle the rocks, you'll be off to the heart of Colorado for two weeks of backpacking. Then you'll learn about camping: how to use a map and compass, wilderness first aid, and how to live and work with a small group.

During the trip, you'll spend one day in the mountains by yourself on a solo. This can be an intense growth experience, and it can also be frightening. Most people remember it as one of the highlights of their trip. After the solo, it's time to get wet on the raging water of the Arkansas river. Maybe the whitest of the white-water rivers, the Arkansas will be an exciting climax for a challenging trip.

 Wem Markham from West Townsend, Vermont went with Interlocken on one of their easier wilderness trips to the Southwest: "It was great. It wasn't exactly a high-impact, roughing-it mountain trip. It was mostly sightseeing, wilderness, and culture, and we hiked San Francisco peaks. We spent a lot of time learning about the Hopi and Navajo cultures. We went around to different places in Utah. We hiked a lot of canyons. I didn't know there were so many canyons."

Although they only took one overnight backpacking trip, the actual camping wasn't that luxurious. "We stayed in tents in campgrounds. No showers. We stopped maybe once a week to use the pools

and the showers. It was kind of a rare occasion, something we cherished." She was particularly impressed with the leaders: "Our leaders were great. They were experienced and they got along with us pretty well. They understood if people were homesick. They would comfort them and talk to them."

Markham's most memorable moment came during the five-day homestay: "Pretty much the first thing I had to do when I walked through the door was slaughter a sheep. It was pretty memorable considering I was a vegetarian. They needed someone to hold it down. And I said, 'I'm a vegetarian' and they said, 'You don't have to actually kill it. You just have to hold it.'" The sheep was slaughtered, but Markham survived and was left with an unforgettable experience.

If you do decide to go on this trip, Markham would advise you to "be prepared for no showers, and don't be afraid to try to meet new and interesting people." An Interlocken wilderness adventure can range from the moderately difficult to extremely difficult. It's an excellent way to see the outdoors and learn about the United States.

Skinner Brothers

Address P.O. Box 859, Pinedale, WY 82941

Phone (800) 237-9138

Costs $500-$2,300

Ages 10-19 (participants for the more popular sessions are grouped by age)

Size of group Fewer than 15 people per group

Lengths of programs 7-28 days

Application deadline Early applications are preferred. They're processed in the order they're received. Two references and an interview are required to be admitted into the program.

Description Wilderness, fishing, and horseback riding in Wyoming

Summary One of the first and most intense of all wilderness programs. Teaches you how to survive in the wild.

History Skinner Brothers Wilderness Camps is one of the pioneers in programs teaching wilderness training. Established in 1956, the program aims to teach you how to survive in the wilderness. The programs are in two levels of difficulty with the harder ones requiring some type of wilderness experience.

A typical program The more difficult program, the Open Mountaineering Session, is four weeks of climbing Gannett Peak (13,804 feet), Wyoming's highest mountain. The program is an actual climb with all the planning involved. For the first few days, you'll figure out the logistics of a twenty-two-day climb, and although the route you pick will be safer than, say, Mt. Everest, you *will* be challenged.

Mountain climbing, as you probably imagine, is an art that takes years to perfect. Luckily, you will be accompanied by one of the highly accomplished Skinner Brothers and other qualified instructors. The program is serious, and although you will have fun, you will have to work for your supper. The entire time that you're on the mountain, you will live off what you can carry and the supplies on the packhorse.

If you have some wilderness experience and want to be challenged, give Skinner Brothers a chance. You will leave able to take care of yourself in the wilds.

George Baker of New York, New York went to Skinner Brothers' First Wilderness Session and enjoyed the experience immensely. The camp was divided into three trips: a survival hike, a horseback expedition, and a rock climbing session. According to Baker, "We had to go out in the wilderness and survive for three days. You couldn't bring a tent, so you had to build your own shelter. If it rained, you had to put leaves on the shelter. No rations were allowed, so you had to kill animals to survive. You couldn't use a regular backpack, so you had to make your own backpack. You even had to make your own needle."

The survival hike was set up to resemble a potentialy life-threatening situation: "The whole thing was as if you were in an airplane, and you crashed miles away from civilization. You might have a rifle, but only one bullet. You had a knife and some string. You had to make traps out of string." Catching food was a challenge, but they had the help of experienced guides: "We caught a snake and some type of field mouse. We made a big stew with everything and some spice to make it better. With the rifle, I got a robin. It was awesome. It tasted like chicken." The guides make sure that the food is edible so nobody gets sick.

The rest of the trip, though not as challenging, is still intense. The horseback ride is through beautiful country over rough roads. The rock climbing is hard work and requires you to belay up a cliff. But the result is worth it, according to Baker: "Even though it was sometimes really tough, afterwards it was cool. It was worthwhile and I will always remember it."

Outward Bound

Address Route 9D, R2 Box 280, Garrison, NY 10524-9901

Phone (800) 243-8520 (914) 424-4000

Costs $995-$2,395 (Financial aid is available based on financial need)

Ages 14-99+ (Separate trips for just high school students and some for anyone 16 and older)

Size of group 8-12

Length of program 8-28 days

Application deadline Early applications are preferred. They're processed in the order they're received.

Description Wilderness/adventure schools in Colorado, Maine, North Carolina, Oregon, and Minnesota

Summary The largest and oldest adventure program in the world. Offers challenging wilderness programs that push you to do things you never thought you could.

History During World War II, German U-boats bombed many British merchant ships. Surprisingly, however, most of the people who were killed were the younger sailors. Educator Kurt Hahn theorized that the younger sailors had not yet developed the fortitude and self-reliance necessary to survive such an experience. He developed a program to increase these skills, and Outward Bound was born. Today, it's the biggest outdoor/adventure program in the world, with fifty Outward Bound centers on five continents. Outward Bound is sometimes used to right kids who are having trouble at school. It is not a sheltered program; you will meet all kinds of people and work with them to meet group goals.

The Program All Outward Bound programs follow a similar format; they all teach you how to survive in the wild. The Canoeing, Boundary Waters Wilderness, Minnesota, at the Voyageur Outward Bound School is fairly typical. You begin with training in the skills necessary to paddle a canoe. You'll learn navigation, paddling and portaging techniques, and water safety. Once you learn these skills, your instructors will give you more freedom to make decisions and to plan the trip.

The setting for the canoe trip is the 1.5-million-acre Boundary Waters Canoe Area Wilderness. With more than 1,200 miles of canoe trails, you won't run out of places to travel. In addition, the area has plenty of opportunity for rock climbing, and there's a ropes course to challenge you.

Depending on the length of the trip, you may get a chance to experience a solo. You will set up a campsite by yourself and get a chance to live in the wilderness alone. Being alone in a site of unparalleled beauty can be an intense growth experience, and many people remember the solos as the highlight of the trip.

Although anyone in decent physical shape can handle these trips, it's a good idea to do some aerobic training (walking, jogging) before you go. An Outward Bound program is a great chance to increase your wilderness skills, face challenges, and have a beautiful wilderness experience.

Andrew Rodney of Ridgewood, New Jersey went with Outward Bound the summer before his sophomore year. He felt that it was intense: "It was great. I felt like I knew the guys at the end—all the instructors too. It was a really great experience, especially for my age. A lot of people have jobs and stuff, but this is better."

There were a lot of activities designed to teach teamwork. In one, the group was sent out on a canoe without paddles to a pond: "Your whole group had to get on the canoe and push themselves out and paddle to this rope with your hands. You had to get everyone over the rope. One at a time we had to get a person over it. They would stand up on the canoe, get over it, and sit back down. We had to all work together."

One of the most memorable parts of the trip was the solo: "We got a really limited amount of food for four days and three nights. They gave you two oranges, two apples, two small bagels, trail mix, and a hunk of cheese. I tried a snail and a crab—uggh—but the seaweed was good. I took it out and left it in the sun and it got crispy. It was really good 'cause it was salty. They also gave us a 2 1/5 gallon jug of water. On the island I was on, there were wild sheep, but I didn't see any. The first night I had fun making my hut. They gave me a tarp, and I made a neat hut. The second day, I started on my solo project. Before I left we had a drawing, and I had to make something for a friend on the trip. I made him a maracas—those Mexican shaking things. I got two sea urchins, stuck a stick through them, put pebbles in them and wrapped a rope around. Then I put shells on it for decoration. It was really cool."

If you do go on an Outward Bound program, Rodney advises that you "be open-minded. You don't know what to expect. At the end I felt great. It was great. I came back thinking I knew those people for so long." He also advises that you bring a few waterproof, throwaway cameras and to pack as lightly as possible.

Sierra Club Outings—Service Trips

Address 730 Polk Street, San Francisco, CA 94139

Phone (415) 923-5522

Costs $200-$300; $50 deposit

Ages 13-17

Size of group 10-20

Lengths of programs 5-9 days

Application deadline Apply early

Description While enjoying the wilderness, participants will work to build trails, remove trash, and restore the areas to their natural beauty.

Summary A great program for someone with some background in camping and hiking and with a strong interest in working to protect the wilderness. Many of the programs will not have roads, showers, toilets, phones, or electricity. Some of the Sierra's many programs are specifically geared toward teenagers.

History Sierra Club National Service Trips is in its thirty-ninth year. In 1996, they will offer over 100 trips in the U.S. for participants to work with the Sierra Club's excellent staff and local and federal government land agencies.

The program It is difficult to describe a typical program since each service trip differs from the next in terms of terrain, the type of work involved, and duration. However, you can get some idea from one of the more popular outings, the Teen Service Trip to John Muir Wilderness in the Sierra Nevadas. The land itself—with rugged alpine country, clear lakes in dense, green forests, peaks of solid granite, and no roads—offers participants the chance to see some unbelievable scenery. The team works on the Goodale Pass Trail, lovingly referred to as "Sierra Club's Own Trail" by many club members. No trail work experience is necessary, but Sierra Club expects you to be ready to move rocks, clear brush, improve drainage, and deal cheerfully with whatever obstacles nature throws in your way.

Service trips aren't only about toil, however. While about five days of the trip are devoted to restoring the trail, the remaining three are free for whatever the group decides to fill them with—hanging out by a pristine lake, climbing rocks, or further exploring the area. Day hiking and exploring must be done in groups of three for safety.

Sierra will send a gear checklist to everyone who signs up for the trip, but, in addition to your backpack and camping gear, you will need a daypack, two one-quart water bottles, sunscreen, sunglasses, and a hat. You won't need cooking gear but you will need a bowl, cup, and spoon. Long pants and two pairs of work gloves are required for trail work, and your hiking boots should be broken in before the trip. It's also a good idea to bring Band-Aids, anti-bacterial ointment, and any medications you regularly take.

Sierra Club Outings—Backpacking Trips

Address 730 Polk Street, San Francisco, CA 94139

Phone (415) 923-5522

Costs $325-$550; $50 deposit

Ages 13-17

Size of group 10-20

Lengths of programs 5-9 days

Application deadline Apply early

Description Challenging backpacking trips throughout North America.

Summary A great program for anyone who loves to feast her eyes and test her mettle. Groups are large but become close-knit over the course of the trips.

History Sierra Club Outings is in its ninety-fifth year. In 1996, they will offer over 350 trips worldwide.

The program Sierra Club Backpacking Trips vary in intensity and duration. The trip through the Emigrant Basin Wilderness Area, on the northern border of Yosemite National Park, is one of the more intense. Designed for somewhat experienced backpackers (but open to some beginners), this is *not* a camping trip. The group hikes about eight or ten miles *every day* from campsite to campsite, using both trail and trailless, cross-country routes. Everything you need to survive in the wilderness is carried on your back, including part of the food supply (each participant starts out with about twenty pounds worth) for the entire group. There are no roads, showers, toilets, phones, or electricity.

If this sounds grueling, it can be, but the trip affords you a sustained look at some of the most astonishing scenery in the world. You also get to climb Tower Peak, a class three mountain which requires that genuine togetherness exist among fellow climbers.

Sierra Club Outings will circulate a gear checklist among accepted applicants, but basic requirements include a large, roomy backpack with room for your part of the central load, a supply of Polypro, Goretex, and wool layers for sudden cold snaps, a warm, well-constructed sleeping bag good for fifteen or twenty degrees above zero, and a good tent with mosquito netting and rainfly. You'll also want an insolite pad or a self-inflating mattress to sleep on, and sturdy, but well-broken-in, hiking boots. You'll need bug repellent. Pack a small, personal first aid kit, as well, with band aids, anti-bacterial ointment, and any medications you need. If you have any medical conditions or allergies, please notify your Sierra Club trip leader in advance.

SPECIALTY CAMPS

Let's say that you're one of those people who loves tennis. You get up every morning and go to school, and while you're there you picture a tennis ball going back and forth in front of the blackboard. Then in the afternoons, you go and hit that furry ball back and forth for a few hours before dinner. Then you snatch a quick meal and head off for the courts again. If you're this obsessed about something or you would like to be this obsessed about something, you should consider attending a specialty camp.

There are specialty camps in a lot of different areas, from sports to the arts to computers. But before you go to one, you should consider whether you want to spend a few weeks doing just one thing.

Now, of course, not all of these camps are so intense. For example, some basketball camps are aimed at people who want to turn professional, while others are for beginners who just like to play the game. The really serious basketball camps, like Eastern Invitational Basketball Camp, bring in college coaches to evaluate your game and to see if you're ready for the next level. If you just want to play, you can go to a more mellow basketball camp where you'll work on skills, and you'll probably have some time to do other things. If you're not sure that this is for you, you might consider one of the other programs in the book. For example, if you know you like oceanography, but you would like to study more than just this, try an on-campus program that offers classes in biology or try Earthwatch (see pages 158-159), a special program in which you work directly with researchers.

Sports Specialty Camps

Big League Sports Camps at Montclair State College

Address P.O. Box 43293, Upper Montclair, NJ 07043
Phone (718) 946-9827
Costs Day Programs $235; Residential Programs $450
Ages 8–21
Size of program 60 participants per session
Length of program 6 days in June–August
Accommodations Dorms
Application deadline Apply a few months in advance to be sure to get in, but they will take registration up to the starting date based on availability
Description Programs emphasizing baseball, tennis, and soccer

Menominee Sports Camp for the Boys

Address 4985 Highway D, Eagle River, WI 54521
Phone (Winter) (800) 236-2267; (Summer) (715) 479-2267
Costs $1,000
Ages 6–16
Class size 150 participants per session
Length of program 13 days in June–July
Accommodations 10–13 boys per cabin
Application deadline Apply a few months in advance to be sure to get in, but they will take registration up to the starting date based on availability
Description Programs emphasizing sports as well as art, wilderness, and academics

The Windridge Tennis and Sports Camps

Address 45 Swift Street, South Burlington, VT 05403

Phone (802) 658-0313

Costs $1,500–$2,600; $400 deposit required

Ages 9–15

Class size 108–168 participants per session

Length of program 3 sessions per camp starting in July

Accommodations Cabins

Application deadline Applications are processed on a first-come, first-served basis as long as space is available

Description Programs emphasizing tennis, soccer, and horseback riding at all skill levels

BASKETBALL

76ers Basketball Camp

Address R.D. 1 Box 1454, Stroudsburg, PA 18360

Phone (Winter) (215) 542-CAMP (Summer) (717) 992-6080

Costs $385

Ages 9–17

Class size 225 participants per session

Length of program 6 days in June–August

Accommodations Cabins

Application deadline Apply a few months in advance to be sure to get in, but they will take registration up to the starting date based on availability

Description Programs emphasizing basketball and other sports

Capital Boys' Basketball Camp

Address The American University, 4400 Massachusetts Ave. NW, Washington, D.C. 20016

Phone (202) 885-3000

Costs Residential programs $310

Ages 6–18

Class size 15–75 participants per session

Length of program 5 days in June–July

Accommodations Dorms

Application deadline Applications are processed at all times based on availability

Description Programs emphasizing basketball and other sports

Ferris State University Girls' Basketball Camp

Address Gerholz Institute of Lifelong Learning, Alumni 113, Ferris State University, 410 Oak Street, Big Rapids, MI 49307

Phone (616) 592-2211

Costs Residential programs $175

Ages 14–18

Class size 100–150 participants per session

Length of program 4 days in June–August

Accommodations Dorms

Application deadline Registration based on availability

Description Programs emphasizing basketball

Jeff Jones Virginia Basketball Camp

Address P.O. Box 3785, Charlottesville, VA 22903

Phone (804) 982-5400

Costs Residential programs $325

Ages 8–18

Class size 300 participants per session

Length of program 5 days in June–July

Accommodations Cabins

Application deadline Applications are processed anytime based on availability

Description Programs emphasizing basketball

Proshot Basketball Camp

Address 142 River Road, Thornhurst, PA 18424

Phone (717) 842-7044

Costs Residential programs $160

Ages 8–18

Class size 20 participants per session

Length of program 3 days in May–October

Accommodations Cabins

Application deadline Rolling

Description Programs emphasizing basketball

St. Mary's College Seahawk Basketball Camp

Address St. Mary's College of Maryland, St. Mary's City, MD 20686

Phone (301) 862-0310

Costs Residential programs $330

Ages 11–16

Class size 50 participants per session

Length of program 5 days in July

Accommodations Dorms

Application deadline Early May

Description Programs emphasizing basketball and other sports

Eastern Invitational Basketball Clinic

Address R.D. #4, Box 4156, Stroudsburg, PA 18360

Phone (717) 992-5523

Costs $390 per weekly session

Ages 16–18

Application deadline Register early, because this one sells out quickly

Description Advanced invitational program emphasizing basketball

Pocono Invitational Basketball Camp

Address R.D. #4, Box 4156, Stroudsburg, PA 18360

Phone (717) 992-6343

Fax (717) 992-5387

Costs Residential programs $350 per week

Ages 14–18

Application deadline Special discount if application is postmarked before January 15

Description Programs emphasizing basketball

FOOTBALL

ASC Contact Football Camps at Shippensburg University of Pennsylvania

Address ASC Football Camps, Inc., Shippensburg University, Shippensburg, PA 17257

Phone (800) 272-7017

Costs Residential programs $499

Ages 8–18

Class size 300–400 participants per session

Length of program 6 days in June–July

Accommodations Dorms

Application deadline Applications are processed anytime based on availability

Description Programs emphasizing contact football staffed by college coaches and NFL professionals

ASC Contact Football Camps at Trinity College

Address ASC Football Camps, Inc., Trinity College, Deerfield, IL 60015

Phone (800) 272-7017

Costs Residential programs $499

Ages 8–18

Class size 300–400 participants per session

Length of program 6 days in June–July

Accommodations Dorms

Application deadline Applications are processed anytime based on availability

Description Programs emphasizing contact football staffed by college coaches and NFL professionals

ASC Contact Football Camps at St. Edward's University

Address ASC Football Camps, Inc., St. Edward's University, Austin, TX 78704

Phone (800) 272-7017

Costs Residential programs $499

Ages 8–18

Class size 200–300 participants per session

Length of program 6 days in June–July

Accommodations Dorm

Application deadline Applications are processed anytime based on availability

Description Programs emphasizing contact football staffed by college coaches and NFL professionals

ASC Kicking Camp at Shippensburg University of Pennsylvania

Address ASC Football Camps, Inc., Shippensburg University, Shippensburg, PA 17257

Phone (800) 272-7017

Costs Residential programs $379

Ages 10–19

Class size 100 participants per session

Length of program 4 days in June–July

Accommodations Dorms

Application deadline Applications are processed anytime based on availability

Description Programs emphasizing football kicking, punting staffed by NFL kickers

ASC Kicking Camp at Trinity College

Address ASC Football Camps, Inc., Trinity College, Deerfield, IL 60015

Phone (800) 272-7017

Costs Residential Programs $379

Ages 10–19

Class size 100 participants per session

Length of program 4 days in June–July

Accommodations Dorms

Application deadline Applications are processed anytime based on availability

Description Programs emphasizing football kicking and punting staffed by NFL kickers

ASC Kicking Camp at St. Edward's University

Address ASC Football Camps, Inc., St. Edward's University, Austin, TX 78704

Phone (800) 272-7017

Costs Residential programs $379

Ages 10–19

Class size 100 participants per session

Length of program 4 days in June–July

Accommodations Dorms

Application deadline Applications are processed anytime based on availability

Description Programs emphasizing football kicking, punting staffed by NFL kickers

Offense-Defense Football Camp

Address Offense-Defense Camps, P.O. Box 1, Easton, CT 06612

Phone (203) 372-8556; (800) 243-4296

Costs Residential programs $540

Ages 8–18

Class size 500 participants per session

Length of program 6 days in June–July

Accommodations Dorms

Application deadline June 15

Description Programs emphasizing football

GOLF

Offense-Defense Golf Camp

Address Offense-Defense Camps, Brewster Academy, Wolfeboro, NH 03894

Phone (203) 256-9844; (800) T-2-GREEN

Costs Day programs $495; Residential programs $750

Ages 10–18

Class size 100 participants per session

Length of program 1 week in July

Accommodations Dorms

Application deadline June 15

Description Programs emphasizing golf, as well as other sports activities, academics, arts, and canoe trips.

JKST Golf and Tennis Schools Summer Camp

Address JKST, INC., P.O. Box 333, Haverford, PA 19041

Phone (610) 265-9401

Costs Day programs $325–$360; Residential programs $660–$735

Ages 10-18

Class size 50 participants per session

Length of program 1 week in June–August

Accommodations Dorms

Application deadline Applications are accepted anytime based on availability

Description Programs emphasizing golf and tennis instruction and workshops.

HORSEBACK RIDING

Allegheny Riding Camp

Address c/o Grier School, Tyrone, PA 16686

Phone (814) 684-3000

Costs $1,850–$3,550

Ages 8–16

Class size 50–100 participants per session

Length of program 20–42 days in June–August

Accommodations Dorms

Application deadline First session begins June 15, second session July 24

Description Programs emphasizing horseback riding as well as other sports activities, arts and wilderness

TENNIS

Carmel Valley Tennis Camp

Address 27300 Rancho San Carlos Road, Carmel, CA 93923

Phone (408) 624-7117; (800) 234-7117

Costs 2-week program $1,350; 1-week program $725

Ages 10–17

Class size 60–70 participants per session

Length of program 2-week sessions and 1-week sessions in June–August

Accommodations Single-sex cabins

Application deadline Early registration gets a discount, but applications are processed up to the day camp starts based on availability

Description Programs emphasizing tennis, as well as other sports activities

Nick Bolletteri Tennis Camps

Address 5500 34th St. West, Bradenton, Florida 34210

Phone (941) 755-1000; (800) USA-NICK

Costs Day program $425; Residential program $595

Ages 8–18

Class size 20–300 participants per week depending on location and season

Length of program 6 days in June–August

Accommodations Dorms

Application deadline 4 weeks prior to arrival; subject to availability

Description Programs emphasizing tennis instruction, mental efficiency training, fitness, and conditioning

Harry Hopman/Saddlebrook International Tennis

Address 5700 Saddlebrook Way, Wesley Chapel, FL 33543
Phone (813) 973-1111
Costs Day program $80; Residential program $660
Ages 9–20
Class size 180 participants per session
Length of program 5 days/6 nights in June–August
Accommodations Condos at a local hotel
Application deadline 2 months in advance; will take last-minute registration based on availability
Description Programs emphasizing tennis

Tennis: Europe

Address 146 Cold Spring Road, Unit 13, Stamford, CT 06905
Phone (800) 253-7486; (203) 964-1939
Fax (203) 967-9499
Costs $2,995–$5,950
Ages 14–18
Class size 13–14 players and 2 instructors
Length of program 26–33 days
Accommodations Hotels
Application deadline Apply early, but applications will be processed anytime depending on availability
Description Tennis tours of Europe; play in tournaments throughout Europe.

Ramey Tennis Schools

Address Our Tennis House, 5931 Highway 56, Owensboro, KY 42301
Phone (502) 771-5590
Costs Day programs $360; Residential programs $480; Tournament camp $895–$1600
Ages 10–18
Class size 4–20 participants per session
Length of program 1–10 weeks in June–August
Accommodations 6–8 students per mobile home
Application deadline Applications processed anytime depending on availability
Description Programs emphasizing tennis, as well as other sports activities and field trips to art and culture events.

Offense-Defense Tennis Camp

Address Offense-Defense Camps, Curry College, Milton, MA 02186
Phone (203) 374-7171; (800) TENNIS-3
Costs Day programs $360; Residential programs $650–$680
Ages 9–18
Class size 160 participants per session
Length of program 1–4 weeks in June–August
Accommodations Dorms
Application deadline June 1
Description Programs emphasizing tennis, as well as other sports activities, field trips to art and culture events, and English as a second language classes.

The Lawrenceville Tennis Camp

Address The Lawrenceville School, Lawrenceville, NJ 08648
Phone (609) 896-0054
Costs $585 per week
Ages 9–18
Class size 95 participants per session
Length of program 5–10 days in June–August
Accommodations Dorms
Application deadline They will process applications anytime, though applying a few months in advance is recommended
Description Programs emphasizing tennis, as well as other sports activities

ICE SKATING

Figure Skating Camp at Lake Placid

Address National Sports Academy at Lake Placid, 12 Lake Placid Club Drive, Lake Placid, NY 12946
Phone (518) 523-3460
Costs $185 per week
Ages 9–18
Class size 30–50 participants per session
Length of program 1 week in June–September
Accommodations Dorms
Application deadline Booked on a weekly basis depending on availability
Description Programs emphasizing figure skating; academic tutoring available

Arts Specialty Camps

ART

Rhode Island School of Design

Address 2 College Street, Providence, RI 02903-2787
Phone (401) 454-6200
Costs Residential programs $3,330
Ages 16–18
Class size 360 participants per session
Length of program 6 weeks in June–August
Accommodations Dorms
Application deadline May 20
Description Programs emphasizing art and design

Carnegie Mellon University Pre-College Program in the Fine Arts

Address 5000 Forbes Ave, Pittsburgh, PA 15213
Phone (412) 268-2082
Costs Residential programs $2,505–$2,715
Ages 15–17
Class size 350 participants per session
Length of program 6 weeks in June–August
Accommodations Dorms
Application deadline May 1
Description Programs emphasizing fine arts as well as architecture, art history and art appreciation

Center for Creative Youth

Address Wesleyan University, Middletown, CT 06459
Phone (203) 685-3307
Costs Residential programs $2900
Ages 14–18
Class size 200 participants per session
Length of program 5 weeks in July–August
Accommodations Dorms
Application deadline April 1
Description Programs emphasizing the arts, career exploration, and leadership training

MUSIC

The Berklee Summer Performance Program

Address Berklee College of Music, 1140 Boylston St., Boston, MA 02215
Phone (617) 266-1400
Costs Day program $1,695; Residential program $2,840; $60 mandatory fee
Ages 15 and older
Class size 500 participants per session
Length of program 7–32 days
Accommodations Dorms
Application deadline July 10
Description Programs emphasizing contemporary music performance, academic areas in music, as well as art programs.

International Music Camp

Address 1725 11th St. SW, Minot, ND 58701

Phone (Winter) (701) 838-8472; (Summer) (701) 263-4211

Costs $180

Ages 10–18

Class size 10–440 participants per session

Length of program 1 week in June–July

Accommodations Dorms

Application deadline June 1

Description Programs emphasizing fine arts, as well as programs for the academically and artistically talented.

Encore Music Camp of Pennsylvania

Address Dept. of Music, Theater and Dance, Wilkes University, P.O. Box 111, Wilkes-Barre, PA 18766

Phone (717) 831-4426 (800) 945-5378

Costs Day programs $250–$610; Residential programs $850–$2120

Ages 10–18

Length of program 2–6 weeks in July–August

Accommodations Dorms

Application deadline May 1

Description Programs emphasizing music, theater, and classical dance

Kinhaven Music School

Address Lawrence Hill Road, Weston, VT 05161

Phone (Winter) (610) 868-9200; (Summer) (802) 824-4332

Costs $1,300–$3,000

Ages 10–18

Class size 60–95 participants per session

Length of program 15–42 days in June–August

Accommodations Dorms

Application deadline A few months in advance is recommended, though they will take registration up to camp start date based on availability

Description Programs emphasizing chamber and orchestral music

National Guitar Summer Workshop

Address Scripps College, Claremont, CT 91711

Phone (203) 567-3736; (800) 234-6479 (in-state)

Costs $500

Ages 12 and up

Class size 125 participants per session

Length of program 1–2 weeks in July

Accommodations Dorms

Application deadline Rolling

Description Programs emphasizing rock and classical guitar

PERFORMING ARTS

French Woods Festival of the Performing Arts

Address RR1 Box 228, Hancock, NY 13783

Phone (Winter) (305) 346-7455 or (800) 634-1703; (Summer) (914) 887-5600

Costs Residential programs $1,895–$4,700

Ages 7–17

Class size 400 participants per session

Length of program 3–9 weeks in June–August

Accommodations Cottages

Application deadline Enrollment begins in September. Some sessions fill in January. Applications accepted anytime based on availability

Description Programs emphasizing performing and visual arts, as well as sports and outdoor activities

Perry Mansfield Performing Arts School and Camp

Address 40755 RCR # 36, Steamboat Springs, CO 80487

Phone (800) 430-ARTS

Costs Residential programs $475–$2450

Ages 8 and up

Class size 25–100 participants per session

Length of program 1–9 weeks in June–August

Accommodations Dorms

Application deadline Rolling

Description Programs emphasizing performing arts, fine arts, outdoor, and sports activities

Point Arts Camp–Musical Theatre and Dance Division

Address University of Wisconsin—Stevens Point, Stevens Point, WI 54481

Phone (715) 346-3982

Costs Residential programs $325

Ages 12–18

Class size 40–60 participants per session

Length of program 1 week in July

Accommodations Dorms

Application deadline June 1

Description Programs emphasizing musical theatre and dance

Stagedoor Manor Performing Arts Training Center and Camp

Address Star Route, Loch Sheldrake, NY 12759

Phone (Winter) (914) 636-8578; (Summer) (914) 434-4290

Costs Residential programs $2,250

Ages 8–18

Class size 245 participants per session

Length of program 3 weeks in June–August

Accommodations Hotel rooms

Application deadline Rolling

Description Programs emphasizing theatre and dance, as well as sports and academic activities

Brant Lake's Dance and Tennis Center

Address Route 8, Brant Lake, NY 12815-9732

Phone (518) 494-2406

Costs Residential programs $2,100–$3,700

Ages 12–17

Class size 42 participants per session

Length of program 3 weeks in June–August

Accommodations Dorms

Application deadline A few months in advance recommended; based on availability

Description Programs emphasizing dance, tennis, arts, and water activities

Boston University Theatre Institute

Address Boston University, 855 Commonwealth Ave. #470, Boston, MA 02215

Phone (617) 353-3390

Costs Residential programs $2,800

Ages 15 and up

Class size 50–65 participants per session

Length of program 6 weeks in June–August

Accommodations Dorms

Application deadline May 1

Description Programs emphasizing theatre arts

Ensemble Theatre Community School

Address P.O. Box 188, Eagles Mere, PA

Phone (Winter) (212) 794-4696; (Summer) (717) 525-3043

Costs Residential programs $2,500

Ages 14–18

Class size 16–20 participants per session

Length of program 6 weeks in June–August

Accommodations Dorms

Application deadline May 1; for early acceptance March 31

Description Programs emphasizing theatre, acting, and music

Water Specialty Camps

NAVAL/SAILING/SCUBA

Culver Summer Naval School

Address Culver Summer Camps, Culver Educational Foundation, 1300 Academy Road #138, Culver, IN 46511

Phone (219) 842-8207; (800) 221-2020

Costs 6 weeks $2,800; 2 weeks $1,100

Ages 11–16

Class size 1,400 participants per session

Length of program 2 weeks for specialty camp

Accommodations Dorms with 2 per room

Application deadline By April 1 is recommended, but they will take registration up to the starting date based on availability

Description Programs emphasizing naval training, horsemanship, aviation, as well as activities and sports, including scuba and snorkeling.

Sail Caribbean

Address 79A Church Street, Northport, NY 11768

Phone (516) 754-2202; (800) 321-0994

Costs $1,750–$5,900

Ages 13–18

Class size 50 participants

Length of program From 10 days to 2, 3, 4, or 5 weeks in July–August

Accommodations Yachts; everyone either has his own berth or sleeps on deck

Application deadline Enrollment is limited, filling in March. Interviews and/or recommendations must accompany application

Description Programs emphasizing sailing, racing, and seamanship

Actionsail/ActionDive

Address Actionquest Programs, P.O. Box 5507, Sarasota, FL 34277

Phone (813) 924-6789

Costs $2,485–$2,985

Ages 13–19

Class size 330 participants per session in 12 different voyages, grouped by age

Length of program 2-, 3-, 5-, and 6-week sessions in June–August

Accommodations Yachts with cabins

Application deadline Applications accepted anytime, though most fill in May

Description Programs emphasizing sailing, scuba diving certification, marine biology, oceanography, live-aboard voyages, and leadership training

Broadreach Scuba Adventures and Training

Address P.O. Box 788, Cary, NC 27512

Phone (919) 467-4272

Costs $2,270–$2,890

Ages 14–19

Class size 10–20 participants per session

Length of program 20–25 days in June–August

Application deadline Rolling

Description Programs emphasizing scuba diving, advanced and specialty dive training, marine biology, kayaking, and sailing

Science Specialty Camps

COMPUTERS

Computer-Ed High-Tech Camp

Address Lasell College, P.O. Box 177, Weston, MA 02193

Phone (617) 933-7681; (800) 341-4433

Costs Residential programs $1,085

Ages 8–17

Class size 140 participants per session

Length of program 13 days in June–August

Accommodations Dorms

Application deadline Applications available in November; first-come, first-serve basis

Description Programs emphasizing computer and space science, technology, art, as well as sports activities

National Computer Camps at Oglethorpe University

Address Atlanta, GA 30304

Phone (203) 795-9667

Costs Residential programs $450

Ages 8–18

Class size 50 participants per session

Length of program 1 week in July

Accommodations Dorms

Application deadline A few months in advance; registration based on availability

Description Programs emphasizing computer science, programming, as well as sports and recreation

National Computer Camp at Santa Clara University

Address Santa Clara, CA 95053

Phone (203) 795-9667

Costs Residential programs $450

Ages 8–18

Class size 50 participants per session

Length of program 1 week in July

Accommodations Dorms

Application deadline A few months in advance; registration based on availability

Description Programs emphasizing computer science, programming, sports, and recreation

National Computer Camps at Sacred Heart University

Address Fairfield, CT 06430

Phone (203) 795-9667

Costs Residential programs $450

Ages 8–18

Class size 50 participants per session

Length of program 1 week in July

Accommodations Dorms

Application deadline A few months in advance; registration based on availability

Description Programs emphasizing computer science, programming, sports, and recreation

National Computer Camp at Ursuline College

Address Pepperpike, OH 44124

Phone (203) 795-9667

Costs Day programs $370; Residential programs $450

Ages 8–18

Class size 50 participants per session

Length of program 1 week in July

Accommodations Dorms

Application deadline A few months in advance; will take registration up to start date based on availability

Description Programs emphasizing computer science, programming, sports and recreation

SCIENCE

Teton Science School

Address Grand Teton National Park, P.O. Box 68, Kelly, WY 83011

Phone (307) 733-4765

Costs Day programs $50 per day; Residential programs $810–$2,075

Ages 12–18

Class size 14–30 participants per session

Length of program 13–42 days in June–August

Accommodations Cabins

Application deadline A few months in advance; will take registration up to camp start date based on availability

Description Programs emphasizing academic course work, field investigation, as well as special areas of interest, sports, and wilderness

OCEANOGRAPHY

Acadia Institute of Oceanography

Address Seal Harbor, ME 04675

Phone (Winter) (207) 439-2733; (Summer) (207) 276-9825

Costs $1,200

Ages 12–18

Class size 40 participants per session

Length of program 2 weeks in June–August

Accommodations Dorms

Application deadline A few months in advance; will take last-minute registration based on availability

Description Programs emphasizing oceanography as well as other sciences, sports, arts and specialty areas such as field research and nature study

Seacamp

Address Box 170 Route 3, Big Pine Key, FL 33043

Phone (305) 872-2331

Costs Residential programs $2,195; 5-day session $180 (extra for scuba)

Ages 12–17

Class size 140 participants per session

Length of program 18 days in June–August

Accommodations Single-sex dorms; 5–7 students per room

Application deadline May 1 recommended; will take registration until one day before session starts based on availability

Description Programs emphasizing marine science studies, oceanography, and other sciences, as well as scuba. Day programs available to students living or vacationing in the area.

SPACE

U.S. Space Camp and Space Academy

Address One Tranquility Base, Huntsville, AL 35807

Phone (205) 837-3400; (800) 63-SPACE

Costs $500 for parent and child; $600 and up per child; $800 per adult

Ages 9–adult

Class size 12 people per team

Length of program 5–8 days

Accommodations Dorm/20–28 children per room; high school students 6 per room

Application deadline 2 weeks in advance, though 4 months in advance is recommended

Description Programs emphasizing study in aerospace science, general science, flight instruction, model rocketry, and pilot activities.

Learning Disability Camps

Landmark School

The Landmark School, located in Prides Crossing, Massachusetts specializes in teaching students who are of average to above-average intelligence but suffering from dyslexia or another form of learning disability. The program is similar to a traditional camp except that it features small classes and one-on-one tutoring aimed specifically at overcoming the learning disability. Its staff, trained in teaching intelligent students with learning disabilities, can pinpoint problem areas and improve the students' language and math skills so that they are better able to excel in a traditional school.

Address Prides Crossing, MA 01965

Phone (508) 927-4440

Cost $3,050–$4,900

Age 8–20

Class size 140–160 participants per session

Length of program 6 weeks in July–August

Accommodations Dorms

Application deadline Applications are processed on a first-come, first-served basis; space is limited

Description Programs emphasizing full academics, half-day options, preparatory summer program, seamanship, marine science, and extracurricular activities

Flight Camp

Florida Air Academy

Address 1950 South Academy Drive, Melbourne, FL 32901

Phone (407) 723-3211

Cost Residential programs $2,400

Age 11–18

Class size 200 participants per session

Length of program 6 weeks in July–August

Accommodations Dorms

Application deadline Applications accepted anytime based on availability

Description Programs emphasizing flight instruction and computers

Culture Beyond
the Petri Dish

4

Culture Beyond the Petri Dish

THE ART OF LEARNING

Remember last year during English class when you were forced to read *The Scarlet Letter* and you had to miss a great movie or set aside reading another book that you actually *wanted* to read? You may have gotten through Nathaniel's masterpiece, but most likely, you looked at it as an assignment, something that had to be done for a grade. Most high schools don't have extensive programs devoted to movies, music, or the visual arts. If you expect to learn about these topics, you're on your own.

Some schools don't stress the need for independent learning. This summer, teach yourself about twentieth-century American poets, Latin American literature, the blues roots of rock and roll, or French film. Choose your own book and read it for pleasure, pick out some great movies to watch on a VCR, visit a museum, or check out some CDs or records from the library. No matter what topic you choose, there's bound to be a song, book, film, or painting about to it.

Be Systematic

The trick is to work steadily. Set up a schedule and stick to it. It's not enough to experience culture willy-nilly; it takes a certain kind of effort to make learning fun and effective.

Keep a Journal

No matter what you decide to do this summer, you might forget some of the details a few years from now unless you write it down. Now, this isn't a big deal if you plan to spend the entire summer sleeping by the pool, but if you do something interesting, you should record it.

Most of us will start a journal and write for maybe a week and then give up. It's tough work, and, unless you establish a regular time every day, you probably won't keep it up. To get started all you'll need is a notebook. If you notice something interesting, make a note of it.

Do a Little Bit Every Day

Later in this chapter, we provide lists of books for summer reading, movies to see, and music to listen to. Pick out the stuff you want to do, add your own selections to it, and then set up a schedule for yourself. It's not important that you keep to the schedule exactly (i.e., "I'll read seventy-five pages of *War and Peace* every day"), but if you have a general order to your summer, you'll find that you accomplish much more.

BOOKS

If we had to suggest one thing that would increase your grades and SAT scores, make you a better writer, a better student, and increase your knowledge of the world, it would be to read as many good books as possible. The summer is a perfect time to go to the library or bookstore and start reading. Many schools will give you a summer reading list, but if your school doesn't do this, check out the one on the following pages. In one summer, you can probably read eight to ten books and be one huge step ahead of your classmates.

Make Merriam Webster Your New Best Friend

While you're reading, try to add to your vocabulary. Watch out for words that you don't know, and if you're anywhere near a pencil, jot them down to look up later. You're going to need these words when you take the PSAT and SAT, so while you're reading, you can increase your vocabulary.

Make a Declaration of Independence

The theme of a kid coming of age—making the leap into the adult world—never wears out.

Bastard Out of Carolina, by Dorothy Allison. The story of a smart and savvy but poor white girl from South Carolina whose troubled family makes growing up even tougher.

I Know Why the Caged Bird Sings, by Maya Angelou. The first part of poet Maya Angelou's life story, this lyrical book tells of her struggles and dreams.

Emperor of the Air, by Ethan Canin. Several of the stories in this collection deal with teenage boys facing their futures.

Invisible Man, by Ralph Ellison. No, it's not science fiction, it's the classic story of a young African American man coming to terms with himself and White society.

In Our Time, by Ernest Hemingway. If you've never read Hemingway, now is the time and this is the book. A collection of linked stories set around the end of World War I.

Steppenwolf, by Herman Hesse. This classic novel is revered by young, alienated, too-smart-for-their-own-good types.

Sula, by Toni Morrison. The complicated friendship between two young African American women is the focus of this novel by the Nobel Prize-winning Morrison.

Catcher in the Rye, by J. D. Salinger. The one and only.

A Boy's Own Story, by Edmund White. A young gay man comes of age.

Travel to Exotic Places

If you're stuck at home in your boring sub-urban life (or if you just need a change of pace from your ultra-exciting life) try a little mind travel.

West with the Night, by Beryl Markham. An inspiring account of the adventures of gutsy female aviation pioneer Markham.

Paddy Clarke Ha Ha Ha, by Roddy Doyle. Ireland in the mid-1960s comes alive in this slice-of-life tale of a ten-year-old boy.

Son of the Circus, by John Irving. A novel about an Indian doctor living in Canada and his travels back and forth across cultures.

Riding the Iron Rooster, by Paul Theroux. An account of an American guy's travels through China.

It's Fun . . . Really

We're not saying that you should pore over boring old classics in some dark library. We think you should pick books to read that are entertaining and at the same time meaningful. In addition, we don't suggest you do all your reading inside. One great thing about books is that they are portable; you can take them anywhere. Take your book with you. Read on the bus and at the beach.

Nobody is going to test you on this stuff, so you might as well have fun with it. Take your time and try to imagine what the characters are feeling; put yourself in their place.

Use Your Imagination

These books have fantastical elements.

Oscar and Lucinda, by Peter Carey. Love, colonialism, commerce, and religion get mixed up with magic in this novel of Australia in the nineteenth century.

One Hundred Years of Solitude, by Gabriel Garcia Marquez. Don't be put off by the title—this exciting book about several generations of a Latin American family mixes folklore, history, and magic.

Dreamquest of Unknown Kadath, by H. P. Lovecraft. If you like Tolkien, you'll love Lovecraft.

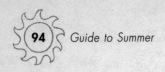

Get Creative

Of course, the obvious places to find books are at the bookstore and the library. But there are some other places that you might want to check out, too:

- *Second-hand bookstores* *They may be dusty, but more often than not you'll find some pretty great stuff at lower prices than at your average bookstore.*

- *Yard sales* *One person's junk is another's treasure; you never know what someone will get rid of for fifty cents.*

- *Sidewalk sales* *The city equivalent of yard sales.*

- *Libraries* *Often, libraries get rid of old copies of their books to update them with more recent editions. Take advantage of this. They may be a bit rag-tag, but the words are still the same.*

- *Your relatives* *Know anyone with a lot of reading material? Maybe they'd be willing to part with a few of their books for a while.*

- *The Salvation Army* *They're not just for cheap vintage wear. SAs accept book donations as well as clothing. It's definitely worth a look.*

- *The trash* *Okay, no one's saying you have to go wading through someone else's chicken bones, but as you're strolling along look to see if someone has tossed out a copy of* The Sun Also Rises. *What the heck, it's free, right?*

- *Churches* *Sometimes churches will have rummage sales or even give books away. Check out your local paper, supermarket, post office, or Laundromat bulletin board for ads.*

- *Schools* *So you might not have planned on entering the halls again until September, but you might want to see if your high school is having any book sales. Schools frequently get rid of their worn-out copies of books in order to buy the more recent editions for the new school year.*

Keep Cool
Here are some hot books set in cool climes.

Smilla's Sense of Snow, by Peter Hoeg. This mystery thriller features plenty of snow and memorable characters.

The Woman Lit by Fireflies, by Jim Harrison. The Upper Peninsula of Michigan, a pretty cool place, is the setting for the title story.

The Shipping News, by E. Annie Proulx. Set on the icy, remote island of Newfoundland, this novel is about a man who needs to find a new life.

One Day in the Life of Ivan Denisovich, by Aleksandr Solzhenitsyn. An historical novel about a soldier's life in Siberia.

The Library

Although we've given you some alternative sources for finding books, the library is certainly one of the best—and cheapest—sources for books. And, if you go on to college you will need to learn how to use the library well, so by using the library to find summer reading material, you will get a head start.

Explore American Cultures
Delve into some of the many cultures that make up America.

Love Medicine, by Louise Erdrich. The first of a beautiful, haunting three-part saga of several generations of a Native American family.

All the Pretty Horses, by Cormac McCarthy. This novel does the American West like no other.

The Joy Luck Club, by Amy Tan. Chinese American mothers and daughters face the transition from China to America in this novel.

Woman Hollering Creek, by Sandra Cisneros. Latino culture is explored in this magical book.

Libraries are especially good for finding nonfiction books. The books are arranged by subject, which means that you can explore an area just by going to the shelves. Let's say, for example, that you want to learn more about World War II. Maybe you have a relative who fought in the war, and you want to find out more about it. What can you do?

Travel in Time
The Alienist, by Caleb Carr. This historical crime novel is set in gritty, turn-of-the-century New York.

Time and Again, by Jack Finney. Time travel at its best.

Neuromancer, by William Gibson. The original cyberpunk novel.

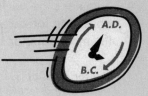

As you know, you can use the library's card catalogue or computer to look up books by subject, author, or title. When you find where the World War II books are, go to the shelves. Libraries' nonfiction books are usually arranged by the Dewey

Get Real

Here are some nonfiction books that will reward your curiosity.

Fear and Loathing in Las Vegas, by Hunter S. Thompson. Madness and mayhem from a smart, zany journalist.

The Hidden Life of Dogs, by Elizabeth Marshall. A must-read for all dog lovers.

Makes Me Wanna Holler, by Nathan McCall. A reporter for the Washington Post tells the story of his journey from the streets to prison to journalism and reflects on the difficulty African American males face in our society.

Being Digital, by Nicholas Negroponte. A professor of media technology talks about the information technology revolution and what it means for the future.

The Diary of Anne Frank. This real diary of a teenage Jewish girl in hiding during the Holocaust will amaze and move you. A new, completely uncut version has just been issued.

decimal system. This system keeps books of the same subject in the same area. So if you look up World War II in the card catalog or computer and find a few books in the same area, go to the shelves and look around. Chances are there are a whole slew of books about the war, and you could spend the whole summer learning about this period of American history. Many students make the mistake of writing down the number of every book they find. Then they go to the stacks and are frustrated when the books aren't there. Just find a few books and start browsing among the stacks.

Be Mysterious

Summer's the perfect time to indulge your obsession for detective fiction, still one of the most popular fictional genres.

A is for Alibi, by Sue Grafton. The first of Grafton's well-known detective novels that work through the alphabet.

Black Betty, by Walter Mosley. African American detective Easy Rawlins hits the streets of L.A.

Dancehall of the Dead, by Tony Hillerman. This novel set in a Native American community won the Edgar award, the highest honor for mystery fiction.

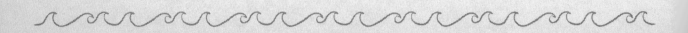

Another great thing about libraries is that you can spend hours just going through the stacks and looking around. You may find a book about a new and interesting subject. You can spend hours in a library, learning on your own and never getting bored. The library is a broad resource with better selections than

Get Ready for College
These books are set on college campuses. Some give you the scoop on what your life will be like; some give you the lowdown on your professors.

Moo, by Jane Smiley. This novel tells about many levels of raucous goings-on at a big Midwestern university.

The Secret History, by Donna Tartt. A clandestine clique at an elite Northeastern college stumbles into trouble.

Nice Work, by David Lodge. An English professor and a corporate industrial type tangle professionally and romantically in this "academic satire."

many bookstores have. The amount of information in your public library is outstanding, and most libraries will order more books from affiliated libraries if they don't have what you need. In addition, many libraries offer seasonal loans for the summer. This means that you can take out several books for the entire vacation.

We're Going to Say it Again

Read, read, read, read. It's the Princeton Review's recommended daily allowance for getting smarter. The knowledge you glean from reading will increase your SAT scores, impress college admissions officers, wow your friends, and, believe it or not, entertain you.

Whole worlds will open up to you this summer if you spend some time with a few good books. From the comfort of your home, or even your beach chair, you can visit so many places. Hit the library and there's no limit to what you can do.

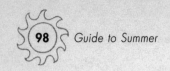

MOVIES

Chances are you've never taken a class on movies in high school. Even though movies are a major part of our culture, most schools leave this part of your education to you. Too bad, because there are some great ones out there, and summer is the perfect time to explore them.

The Princeton Review's Guide to Becoming a Tape Head

There are more movies than what's in the "New Releases" section of your video store. On pages 99-112, we provide a list of 91 films that will definitely be worthwhile for your summer vacation. We have organized these in different categories so that if you find out that no matter what you're interested in, you'll definitely find some must-sees.

Although a good movie, like a good book, might take more effort to absorb, you will find the time spent worthwhile. Make watching these movies an excuse for socializing. Organize a small film festival: invite your friends, make popcorn, and spend some time discussing the films. Here are some themes to explore:

- *Find out what recent movies are remakes and watch the original versions.*

- *Have a night devoted to one star. Make it a Katharine Hepburn or John Travolta night, rent four or five movies, and let the marathon begin.*

- *Devote a night to one director. If you don't know any, pick one of your favorite movies and find out who the director is. Chances are he or she has made some other great films.*

- *Find some films that originally came from books, short stories, or plays. Read the lit and compare it to what you see.*

- *Rent by country. Take a night out to watch films made in Ireland, China, France, or Italy.*

- *Pick a historical era. Curious about the Civil War or the civil rights movement? There have been some intense, evocative films made about these events.*

- *Ever wonder what influenced some artists to do what they do, or what their lives might have been like? Try picking up a few movies about a famous musician or artist, like Charlie Parker or Vincent van Gogh.*

The Search Mission

You can find a wide variety of films in two locations: libraries and video stores. Libraries are free and usually have a few classic films, but in general their hours and selection are not very flexible. Video stores give you a larger variety and are more convenient than libraries. They are usually cheap, but watch out; some stores are limited to only the most popular films. Although some of the bigger chains

Coolin' Off

The films in this category are all good to watch on a hot day.

Never Cry Wolf (1983)—A gorgeous film based on the true story of a lone scientist by the name of Farley Mowatt who was sent by the U.S. government to the Arctic to study the behavior of wolves. The truly determined Mowatt gets over his head in this excellent adventure with spectacular snowy landscapes, a pack of wolves, and a wise Inuit.

The Thing (1982)—A remake of the 1951 original, this is one of the scariest, most intense films you will ever see. If the icy setting of Antarctica doesn't cool you off, maybe the nastiness these researchers pull up from under the ice will chill your bones.

Ice Station Zebra (1968)—Rock Hudson is a submarine commander on a mission to the North Pole, unaware of the presence of a Russian spy who will make his mission treacherous. Cold weather, Cold War, cool movie.

Better Off Dead (1985)—A summer romance goes to hell when John Cusack's girlfriend falls for the captain of the ski team. Of course he'll go to extreme lengths to win her back. The scene in which the two young lovers fall for each other during a summer picnic is enough reason to rent the movie. If you're pining for winter sports after you get sick of the beach, this film also boasts great ski sequences.

(Blockbuster, for example) have a large selection, you might not live in a large, metropolitan area so you might have to find some smaller video store and watch more obscure films. Call around to stores and ask if they have a specialty.

Read Between the Subtitles

Watching films from other countries is a great way to learn about other cultures. However, be aware that these films often come with subtitles. You may already be a foreign-film buff and have no problem with reading the English translation during a movie, but if you're not, don't be turned off by subtitles. There are amazing

Bored? Try Some Explosions.

Sometimes, despite the fact that it's nice and sunny outside, we just get bored. Well, if that's the case, consider watching one of these films to get your heart pumping. And yes, each one of the films below promises some good pyrotechnics.

Aliens (1986)—After defeating just one of the nasty critters in the first film, Sigourney Weaver accompanies a detachment of space age marines to a planetary colony that might have encountered the alien. Sure enough, several hundred drooling aliens have taken over the colony. Scary and exciting, with about five climaxes and many explosions (even a nuclear one). This film will leave you exhausted.

Die Hard (1988)—Useless subplots abound but you can easily forget that they're even there, because the rest of the movie is packed full of great action and special effects. Alan Rickman makes such an enjoyable villain you almost want to root for him. One very large explosion qualifies it for this category.

Lethal Weapon (1987)—Slick, fast, and trashy—the archetype of the summertime, Hollywood action film. Mel Gibson and Danny Glover have a good screen camaraderie and if you've seen one of the Lethal Weapon films, you've seen them all, so why not start with the original? Lots of guns and one big explosion.

Predator (1987)—A merging of several genres—it's a war picture, action film, and sci-fi film, all at the same time. Predator is a lot of fun, and if the authentic jungle locations don't remind you of how hot it is outside, you've been in the air-conditioning too long. And what would summer be without an Arnold Schwarzenegger movie? Probably a little more peaceful. Lots and lots of guns, lots of explosions, and one alien-generated blast that seems to have nuclear potential.

Raiders of the Lost Ark (1981)—The first and absolute best. Harrison Ford is archeologist and adventurer Indiana Jones, and, when he's not teaching, he's battling snakes, Nazis, and even the power of God! No matter where you watch this movie, it can't be as hot as the desert where our hero discovers the lost ark. Great stunts, action, and special effects all the way, and several large explosions, including one detonation by the Big Man himself.

Robocop (1987)—It's summer in futuristic Old Detroit, and a brave police officer is about to get blown to smithereens by one of the baddest villains in action movie history. His body is used to create a law enforcement cyborg who is lethally efficient but haunted by the memory of his human life. Ultra-violent and intelligent, Robocop gives you a lot more than you bargained for, including some bitingly funny social satire. More guns than you can count, several explosions, and some toxic waste that really doesn't agree with one unfortunate villain.

movies being made all over the world, but you will get much more out of these films if you pay attention to the details. In addition to following the plot, you should look at the way in which the films are made. Sometimes the smallest details tell you a lot about what's happening, or what will occur in the story later. Such things as a cigarette lighter on a table with someone's initials on it, a looming storm, or the decorations in an apartment may seem unimportant, but can give you clues to the storyline, and the characters as well.

Film, just like other art forms, wants to communicate emotion or plot through many means. While you're watching, try to get beyond the story, and figure out why and how it's told.

Keep a Journal

It's not enough to watch good films. You should give yourself time to think about them too. Try keeping some kind of film journal. Keep track of what you watch, and write a brief synopsis of what happened in every film. If you find someone that you really like in the film—maybe an actor or director—mark down his or her name.

This summer is a chance to explore some of the great motion pictures. After watching them, you'll find that you're much more discerning. Good films, like any other work of art, can be enormously enriching—enabling you to see the world in a more mature and thoughtful way.

 Lee Elliott, of New York, New York spent the summer before his eleventh grade watching movies. He didn't have a job, and he didn't leave the city: "I just went to every movie in town with a friend of mine. It was hot, and the theaters were air-conditioned." He also rented every movie he could: "Counting the movies we saw on video, we saw probably sixty movies. We did see some movies twice. We would stay and see a movie again or convince our parents to see it."

Elliott's favorite film was a foreign film: "The best movie we saw was The Fourth Man. After we'd seen every Hollywood movie we could, we decided to see a foreign film. When we saw The Fourth Man, it freaked us out totally. It was a very adult film. It was made by a Dutch filmmaker, who has since made films in the U.S.—the guy who made Robocop and Total Recall—but these were different from his earlier films. The Fourth Man is about a gay novelist on a lecture circuit and he's obsessed with Christianity. He runs into a woman and uses her to get to her boyfriend. He becomes convinced that she's a witch when he realizes that her past three husbands have met with weird deaths."

Elliott advises that if you're going to rent movies you try ones you've never seen before: "We didn't think we'd like the foreign films, but they were the best movies we saw that summer. You should take chances and try movies that you wouldn't think you would like."

Fun and Games

An integral part of summer is sporting events. If you find yourself unable to participate for some reason, you can always watch sports. You can also check out any of these films about sports and warm, summer weather.

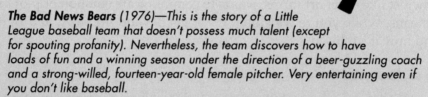

The Bad News Bears (1976)—This is the story of a Little League baseball team that doesn't possess much talent (except for spouting profanity). Nevertheless, the team discovers how to have loads of fun and a winning season under the direction of a beer-guzzling coach and a strong-willed, fourteen-year-old female pitcher. Very entertaining even if you don't like baseball.

Breaking Away (1979)—The summer is rapidly approaching and four college-aged friends are trying to decide what to do with the rest of their lives while being heckled by some cruel students at a nearby college. Among the group of friends is a lovelorn bicycle enthusiast who wants to compete in a team bicycle race to gain some respect and, more importantly, the adoration of some coeds. Regardless of your feelings about bicycling, this film will grab you and remind you of some of the things summer is all about.

Bull Durham (1988)—Some people say summer and baseball go together. If you agree then Bull Durham is the film for you. Kevin Costner, Tim Robbins, and Susan Sarandon make this story of a minor league baseball team and its trials enjoyable.

The Longest Yard (1974)—This is one funny football movie. Burt Reynolds plays a washed-up football pro who gets thrown in jail. Once in, he encounters a manipulative warden who has formed a semi-pro football team out of his guards. When he asks Burt to form an opposing team consisting of inmates, the comedy and the bone-crunching game come to life.

North Dallas Forty (1979)—Possibly, the best football movie ever made. Serious and funny at the same time, North Dallas Forty examines labor abuse within the NFL. It also offers some great football sequences. After you see it, you'll be waiting for fall to come around to get back to the gridiron.

Party Time!

It's summer time, so sleep late and relax. Of course, with all this free time, you'll want to try to fit in as many parties as you can before you have to buckle down again. The films in this category depict some of the wildest, funniest, and best party movies of all time. Naturally, they're all comedies and they capture that aspect of summer which everyone should cherish: hanging out with your friends and having a great time.

Animal House (1978)—The college party film of all time. Fraternity high jinks and more fraternity high jinks, *Animal House* is about as crude as a comedy gets and that's precisely why it's funny. Plenty of laughs, lots of fun, a great soundtrack, and the late, great John Belushi make this a winner.

Fandango (1985)—Five college friends take a road trip the summer after graduation for one last hurrah before entering real life. The final destination is the wedding of one of their best friends and his college sweetheart, but getting there, with the help of one seriously spaced out airplane pilot, is a lot of fun.

Fast Times at Ridgemont High (1982)—One of the best movies about high school ever made, thanks mostly to Sean Penn as the zonkered Jeff Spicoli and Spicoli's nemesis, the teacher, Mr. Hand. Very funny, very honest, and a real good time for everyone who's ever been to high school and had to face the summer after it's all over.

House Party (1990)—When high school students Kid 'N Play have a house to themselves it can only mean one thing—it's time to have a party. Good soundtrack, great dancing scenes, and a lot of good laughs make this a very enjoyable summer movie.

Rock and Roll High School (1979)—The Ramones dominate the soundtrack of this high school movie classic. Loud, boisterous fun that makes you feel like goofing off, which is a healthy pastime in the summer.

Not Quite Summer Camp

The heat gets to people. Weird things happen under the sun's powerful influence that probably wouldn't have otherwise. Well, maybe some of the characters in these movies would have done them anyway, but the summer heat that surrounds them only makes matters worse. Summer isn't always full of carefree days.

Cape Fear (1991)—Martin Scorcese tried something a little different with this remake of the 1962 film of the same name. It's hot and touristy in sunny Florida, but one of the tourists isn't looking for the perfect tan; he's looking for the perfect revenge on the lawyer who sent him to jail fourteen years earlier. What would otherwise be an uneventful summer for star Nick Nolte's family turns into a nightmare when an evildoer played by Robert De Niro shows up. Starts out strong and begins to unravel quickly towards the end, but the performances of all the leads compensate.

Do the Right Thing (1989)—A heat wave is hitting Brooklyn and the racial tensions begin to boil as the sun grows hotter. Arguably Spike Lee's best film, Do the Right Thing captures a city heat wave's intensity quite well and the story, which builds up to a racially charged riot, is tragically played out. The film's climax leaves room for plenty of discussion.

Dog Day Afternoon (1975)—On a hot summer day in Brooklyn, two men (Al Pacino and John Cazale) attempt to rob a bank. What the robbers had intended to be a simple heist turns into a major incident. Pacino holds hostages, tries to keep his bizarre partner in crime from doing anything rash, and negotiates with the police, all to raise the money for his male lover's sex-change operation. Sound incredible? Well, it's based on a true story.

The Emerald Forest (1985)—An engineer is hired to build a dam on the waters of the Amazon. One day, while his son wanders around the site being razed for the dam, the child is kidnapped by a primitive tribe. Dad spends the next ten summers trying to find him in the jungle. Implausible, but it's a good adventure set in a beautiful location with an environmental message as well.

Hope and Glory (1987)—In this British film, with the entire country suffering the effects of German bombing raids, young children of a neighborhood find the war a grand adventure. Richly detailed and bittersweet, Hope and Glory is an original look at World War II through the eyes of a young boy who is never happier than when the summer comes to an end and the state of world war has caused his school to shut down.

Key Largo (1948)—Summertime isn't always sunny, and in Key Largo it isn't always a picnic either. Humphrey Bogart stars in this suspenseful film about a gangster who takes over a hotel in the Florida keys during a tropical storm and holds all of the vacationing guests hostage.

Thelma and Louise (1991)—It's summertime in the middle of America, and two female friends decide to take a road trip to forget their responsibilities and the men in their lives. Things start out fine until they get into a little bit of trouble with an idiotic male and his unwanted sexual advances. Things get worse, and then they get much worse, or better, depending on how you look at it.

Total Inanity

There are days during the summer when you just don't do anything. Why? Not because it's too hot or your bike is broken, but because you can. If you find yourself on one of these rare and glorious days, and you really want all brain activity inside your skull to reach a complete stop, then view any of the following films. Warning: viewing any of these films back to back could be hazardous to your hypothalamus.

Ace Ventura, Pet Detective (1994)—Jim Carrey went straight to the top after this ludicrous movie about the pet detective who is hired to track down the Miami Dolphins' missing mascot. So stupid, it's almost authentically bizarre, but once you've adjusted, you'll have a really good time. The EKG barely registers during this one.

Airplane (1980)—The slapstick, in-your-face, stupid joke writing/directing team known as Zucker-Abrahams-Zucker came up with the last word in disaster film spoofs with Airplane. Just about everything under the sun is lampooned in this hysterically silly movie. Be sure to listen closely to the announcements over the PA system in the airport.

The Kentucky Fried Movie (1977)—Inspired by the comedy sketches of the Zucker-Abrahams-Zucker team (see a trend here?), this movie spoofs everything from the evening news to kung-fu films to new age self-help albums in such an outrageous manner that you're bound to laugh at its audacity. Guaranteed to offend everyone and leave them smiling with no permanent brain damage.

The Man With Two Brains (1983)—Steve Martin is a scientist who is married to the extremely desirable Kathleen Turner, but, as he discovers, she is a "scum queen." All is not lost, however, as he soon finds a new love in the form of a shapely female brain. He spends the rest of the picture looking for a body to fit her into. If you had two brains, one wouldn't forgive the other for the experience, but both would laugh as their higher functions were numbed.

Meatballs (1979)—Bill Murray is a counselor at Camp Sasquatch where not even Ghengis Khan would have had a chance at controlling the kids. Talk about goofing around during the summer, here it is, in all of its inane splendor.

Naked Gun (1988) and/or *Naked Gun 2 1/2* (1991)—The Zucker-Abrahams-Zucker team strike again! These films are barely distinguishable from each other, and you won't remember which one made you laugh harder, but they deliver a lot of belly laughs. Super-idiot police detective Frank Drebin is on the case, so everyone better watch out or they'll be tangled up in his web of utter stupidity. If you can make it through the opening credit sequence of the sequel without laughing, you should go see a doctor.

One Crazy Summer (1986)—From Savage Steve Holland, who first made Better Off Dead (recommended elsewhere), One Crazy Summer is a lot like the former, but not quite as fresh or clever. Nevertheless, it still has several real laughs. Thus, it gets dumped in this dubiously honorable category.

Summer in the Twilight Zone

On lazy, summer days, the mind wanders and strange thoughts can come to us. Anyone who has been on a summer camping trip can tell you that things can get weird fast. Well, here's a list of films for what we'll call "the twilight zone."

Brazil (1985)—Combine George Orwell's 1984 with A Clockwork Orange and The Jetsons and you've got something approximating the visually dazzling, black comedy that is Brazil. Bureaucracy has gone completely out of control in this look at the future. One man tries to hold on to his dreams and nearly finds salvation in a renegade repair man, played by Robert De Niro. A way-out movie with plenty of imagination and social satire, Brazil may leave you with mixed feelings about working for a large corporation.

Close Encounters of the Third Kind (1977)—It's summer in Wyoming, and a single mother is about to get some strange, brightly lit visitors who have a great deal of interest in her son. Steven Spielberg's sci-fi classic remains a story well told that is sometimes frightening, sometimes funny, and sometimes too sentimental, but it's a winner all the way. It'll keep you watching the clear skies at night.

Fitzcarraldo (1982)—It's a long hot summer in the Amazon, and one man would like to establish a trade route through the nearly impenetrable terrain. His boat reaches an unnavigable stretch of river, so he decides to carry the boat over a mountain to the other side (all the while traveling through hostile tribal territory). Yes, the man is obsessed, and that is what this mesmerizing film is about—obsession. No matter what you're doing this summer, you'll sure be glad you're not hauling a big boat over a mountain for Fitzcarraldo.

Heavenly Creatures (1994)—A hypnotic film from New Zealand based on a gruesome true story, it tells the story of two New Zealand schoolgirls who develop a disturbing friendship. They spend a summer together, building solid walls of fantasy around themselves, entering a world no one else comprehends. They go stark raving mad. A fascinating film that will have you glued to the screen.

Local Hero (1983)—In this British film, an oil company representative is sent to a Scottish coastal village in order to purchase land for his company. The fair summer weather and the quirky inhabitants begin to change his way of thinking in this offbeat, finely detailed satire that definitely feels like it's coming from a different, somewhat nicer world.

Withnail and I (1987)—The 1960s are coming to a close and two friends, both unemployed actors, decide to get away from it all by taking the equivalent of a summer weekend in the country. Fear of the end of the decade of love, Withnail's indulgences, a poacher who keeps the eels he catches down his pants and an eccentric and quite homosexual uncle, all serve to undermine the relaxing weekend. Wonderfully written and not of the norm, Withnail and I is full of funny and bittersweet moments.

The Muse of Summer

Summer arts and crafts classes just aren't inspiring you? How about spending a night with one of these incredibly talented people? They may have lived their lives a bit on the wild side, but hey, isn't that why we created the term "artistic freedom"?

Vincent and Theo (1990)—So why did that guy cut his ear off? Why is his work on every wall, coffee mug, and T-shirt now, but nobody really seemed to think he was so great when he was alive? Find out in this intense look at the lives of the great artist Vincent Van Gogh and his brother Theo.

Camille Claudel (1988)—The story of the French sculptress who pursued her art as intensely as she pursued her love of the sculptor Auguste Rodin. Eventually, the mud and the man made her go mad—but in the meantime she was model, muse, and maker of some incredible works of art.

Bird (1988)—Directed by Clint Eastwood, this film takes you through the sad but amazing life and career of jazz saxophonist Charlie Parker, often credited as one of the musicians who revolutionized the jazz scene during the 1940s. Bird doesn't try to paint a rosy picture. It shows not only Parker's musical brilliance, but his demise into a world of drug addiction as well.

Barfly (1987)—So you want to be a writer, eh? The glamour, the fame, the fortune . . . well, not in the case of Charles Bukowski. Not if he had his way, anyway. Bukowski made being a brilliant but crazed drunk an art all its own. He did it all with a smile. Barfly portrays Bukowski at his lowest and his highest moments. After the film, you just might be running to the bookstore to see what this guy was all about.

Impromptu (1991)—The story of writer George Sand, the controversial woman whose clothing choice (she only wore "men's" attire) and pursuit of Chopin (played by Hugh Grant) made her famous for her lifestyle as well as her writing.

Sid and Nancy (1986)—All hail the king and queen of the punk scene. The story of The Sex Pistols' Sid Vicious and groupie Nancy Spungen takes you from the beginning of their reign to the end—with more drugs and debauchery than some can handle. And, of course, the background music isn't to be overlooked. After The Sex Pistols hit the 1970s punk scene, things were never the same.

Coal Miner's Daughter (1980)—Sissy Spacek stars in this bio of country singer Loretta Lynn. The story takes you from Lynn's poor, rural beginnings to super-stardom (and, of course, all the problems that inherently seem to come along with such rising fame). Tommy Lee Jones does a great job playing her manager/husband and Spacek won an Oscar for her performance.

Henry and June (1990)—Based on the diary entries of writer Anaïs Nin, this film takes you through Paris in the early 1930s and her love affair with Henry Miller and infatuation with his wife, June. After watching the film, you just might want to check out the book of the same title (the actual diary entries of Nin).

Once Upon a Time...

In addition to catching up on some reading this summer, you might also want to check out the film versions of some of your favorite books and stories.

The Dead (1988)—This is the beautifully adapted film version of James Joyces' short story of an Irish family set in 1904. The seemingly happy scene is a Christmas party full of friends and family with an abundance of food, drink, and belly-shaking laughter. Eventually, though, we begin to see that things aren't exactly ideal; behind the smiling faces of our hosts lurk secrets and sad tales, tied up in a big bow of discontent.

The Unbearable Lightness of Being (1988)—In Czechoslovakia during 1968, troops invaded the city of Prague in the name of the now-defunct Soviet Union. Using the invasion as a backdrop, this is Milan Kundera's story of a young doctor who avoids dealing with his cheating heart and the grim political situation which surrounds him. Eventually, when his life falls into political and personal turmoil, he must decide where his loyalties lie.

Circle of Friends (1995)—Ever feel like you're living a dual life—one for your parents and one for your friends? Maeve Binchy's story of a young Irish girl trying to do right by her folks and her pals will definitely hit home. Set in the Irish countryside and Trinity College, Dublin, this story has the ingredients for a good night in front of the television with your friends. If you want to end up your evening with a big, goofy smile on your face, rent this one.

A Room with a View (1985)—A young woman is coming of age and traveling through Florence—unfortunately for her, she's also being chaperoned. This British film based on E. M. Forster's novel is a lesson in dealing with propriety and manners while trying to fall in love.

Like Water for Chocolate (1992)—This Mexican folklorish, romantic tale set in the early twentieth century, will not only make you want to fall in love, it'll make you pretty hungry too. In it, a beautiful, young woman is trying to break out from her mother's iron grasp and into the arms of the man she loves. In the meantime, she consoles herself in the kitchen by cooking up dishes that do more than just fill the stomach—they seem to cast quite a spell over everyone and everything. Based on Laura Equivel's exquisite novel.

Last Exit to Brooklyn (1989)—Not for the weak of heart, this intense, gritty, violent movie takes place on the mean streets of Brooklyn in 1952. If you're one for happy endings, it isn't for you. But if you can deal with some pretty heavy topics, you might want to check out this German film of the young and the hopeless. (Book by Hubert Selby, Jr.)

Of Mice and Men (1992)—This is the most recent adaptation (there have been several) of John Steinbeck's classic. You might have read this in school or on your own, and if it made you a little misty on the page, you'd better stock up on the tissues when you sit down to watch it. It's a killer.

Little Women (1933)—Not that there was anything wrong with Winona Ryder's interpretation of Jo, but come on, we're talking Katherine Hepburn here. This was the first film adaptation of Louisa May Alcott's warm story of four sisters growing up in nineteenth-century America—and definitely the best.

Growing Pains

Things can change pretty fast in life. And sometimes when September hits, you realize that you're just not the same person who left those halls a few months ago. Before you head back to the books, why not catch a few flicks about, well, growing up?

Flamingo Kid (1984)—Matt Dillon is a cabana boy for the summer at an upscale beach club. He is initially dazzled by the lives of the people he serves and disenchanted by the working-class lifestyle of his own family. While he spends the summer giving towels to wealthy poolside loungers, he falls in love, becomes a card shark, and comes to see that maybe his family isn't so bad after all.

Heathers (1989)—Popularity and human decency are explored in this twisted morality tale starring Winona Ryder and Christian Slater. The two characters set out to destroy the hierarchical high school social system by killing off the ruling class (look for Shannen Doherty as one of the incredibly bitchy Heathers). It's gets a little gruesome, but it's a lot of fun.

The Last Picture Show (1971)—Growing up in a dusty, one-movie-theater town proves difficult for Jeff Bridges and Cybill Shepherd. Shot in black and white, this is the story of how two high school sweethearts deal with the expectations of post-graduation in small-town Texas.

Romeo and Juliet (1968)—Although there are several film versions of Shakespeare's classic story, this is one of the better ones. What can we say? It's the ultimate coming-of-age, albeit tragic, story. Boy meets girl, girl and boy fall in love, boy's and girl's parents forbid relationship, girl and boy commit suicide. It's a wipeout.

Dogfight (1991)—It's 1963 in San Francisco, and River Phoenix is about to ship off for Vietnam. He and a few other war-bound marines make a cruel bet that involves bringing the ugliest date to a party for later that evening. However, when Phoenix's "ugly duckling" learns of the prank, he learns a big lesson about love, friendship, and human kindness.

Summer Swashbucklers, Thieves, and Knaves

It is possible to get bored during the summer no matter what you're doing. You might even find yourself daydreaming of sunny places where you could get into some kind of trouble. If you ever dreamt of fighting knights, hunting for treasure, or having grand adventures during the summers of your youth, than the following films would probably be just what you'd like to watch some slow, summer evening.

Excalibur (1981)—They should have simply stopped making films about the middle ages after the release of this British film. The legend of King Arthur comes brilliantly, violently, and erotically to life in this medieval epic of chivalry, honor, sorcery, love, and betrayal. Beautifully filmed and completely engrossing, it will make you long to take a walk in the woods and contemplate the time of dragons.

The Great Train Robbery (1979)—In this British film, Sean Connery stars as a sly thief (circa 1860) attempting to pull off the largest heist in history by robbing a shipment of gold, as the title implies, from a moving train. Good period detail, clever dialogue, and scenic English countryside provide the backdrop for a well-plotted robbery and some great stunt work.

Monty Python and the Holy Grail (1975)—A British film that spoofs some of the other films in this category as well as the entire Arthurian legend. Capitalism and morality get trashed along the way in this lunatic film from the infamous Monty Python comedy troupe. A funny way to beat the heat.

The Adventures of Robin Hood (1938)—Absolutely not the movie starring Kevin Costner. This is the one and only, the original, starring Errol Flynn, who's archery and fencing skills put Costner's to shame. A rousing adventure film with plenty of swashbuckling and a truly exciting finale. Check it out.

The Three Musketeers (1974) and *The Four Musketeers* (1975)—Absolutely not the movie starring all those guys like Kiefer Sutherland. Andre Dumas' classic tale is given the royal treatment with a gorgeous production that has fantastic fight scenes, some great comedy, and even some tragedy all expertly mixed together. The sequel, which was actually shot at the same time as the first film, is equal to the original in every respect.

The Treasure of the Sierra Madre (1948)—A classic adventure of three offbeat treasure hunters and their quest for the big score. Excellent atmosphere and a good look at the influence of greed on people. You'll never forget it, and, if you think you're hot, just imagine working in the desert like these guys.

Finally, if you're still feeling like your summer needs more adventure, try any of the following James Bond movies: **Dr. No**, **Goldfinger**, **Thunderball**, **You Only Live Twice**, **Live and Let Die**, **The Spy Who Loved Me**, and **For Your Eyes Only**. We think they're the best of the series and they show some of the best vacation spots in the world.

The Summer of Our Discontent

Despite the best laid plans for a great summer vacation or experience, things can go very wrong and it's always a real bummer. After you watch any of the following films, even your worst summer experience should seem like a picnic. These movies definitely show you how not to spend your time during the summer.

City Slickers (1991)—Four middle-age buddies in varying degrees of dissatisfaction with their lives take a summer trip to a cattle ranch for two weeks of the cowboy life. They're horribly inept at first and come under the scrutiny of a tough hombre named Curly, but everything works out in the end. Funny and sentimental, this is a good summer picture that will, if anything, make you glad to be young.

Jaws (1975)—Are you afraid of the ocean? Well, if you're not, you probably will be after seeing this Steven Spielberg classic. The peaceful summer community of Amity is terrorized by a massive great white shark that likes to eat dogs, kids, young women, boats, and just about everything that gets in front of its mouth. With some truly scary moments and great performances by all the leads, you will be on the edge of your seat, but you sure won't want to vacation in Amity anytime soon.

Knife in the Water (1962)—A young couple are off for a romantic, carefree sailing trip in this Polish film. Feeling happy and benevolent, they pick up a student hitchhiker on the way to the marina. Three definitely becomes a crowd. Very tense and involving, it'll keep you looking over your shoulder the next time you have an opportunity to sail a boat.

National Lampoon's Vacation (1983)—The Griswald family's summer road trip across the nation would probably have been a fine idea if Chevy Chase weren't so inept, accident prone, and distracted by fellow motorist Christie Brinkley. There are parts of a family vacation that we all dread, but after you see this movie, you probably won't mind them anymore.

The River Wild (1994)—Mom, Dad, and son decide take a week out of the summer to do some serious white-water rafting that will hopefully improve and secure their familial bonds. They make friends with some other rafters who turn out to be a very negative bunch and spoil everyone's fun. Kevin Bacon is surprisingly good as the bad guy, and this Deliverance-meets-Murphy Brown-story only goes to show that the family that kills together, stays together. Not a very relaxing vacation.

Romancing the Stone (1984)—Shy, lonesome writer Kathleen Turner journeys to sunny Colombia to help out her sister who's in big trouble. On her way to Cartagena things get worse and she experiences the furthest thing from a vacation that you could imagine. Danny De Vito is on hand as a rather slimy grifter and provides some good laughs.

Stand By Me (1986)—The summer's coming to an end and four kids are trying to come up with something to do to spend their time. When news spreads that a dead body was spotted a few miles up the train tracks, the kids decide to go camping to find the corpse. Now, doesn't that sound like fun? A good film about childhood friends, bullies, the summer before junior high, and a dead body.

Summer Lovin'

The institution of the summer affair is as old as summer vacation, and these films all take their own twist with this theme. Just about all of these films make great date movies too, if you're looking to start a summer romance of your own.

The African Queen (1951)—Filmed on location in Africa, this classic features the great pairing of Humphrey Bogart and Katharine Hepburn as a mismatched couple that takes a boat downriver to escape the dangers of World War I. Along the way, as they battle Germans and each other, they fall in love and have one hell of an adventure. This film also contains one of the most hilarious marriage ceremonies you'll ever see.

American Graffiti (1973)—It's the summer between high school graduation and freshman year of college in 1962. High jinks and attempted romance abound, and, though it is set in a particular time period, anyone who has ever been eighteen can relate to this often funny, often biting summer picture. This is also the film George Lucas made before traveling to a galaxy far, far away for Star Wars.

Grease (1978)—Are you a beauty school drop-out? Do you yearn for your dreamboat listening to Frankie Valli records? Do you wish you raced hot rods in the 1950s? Well, the people in this movie do! And they sing and dance too! Summer lovers John Travolta and Olivia Newton-John dance their way through this wacky musical that is the height of kitsch and very infectious. Fun all the way through, this film knows very well that it is a silly, silly movie.

Gregory's Girl (1981)—An endearing Scottish film about a young man who falls for the girl who takes his place on the soccer team. Gregory, and all of his friends, are so interested in meeting girls that one of them decides to hitchhike to a town 100 miles away where the ratio of women to men is supposed to be 4:1. A look at what summer romance is like across the ocean.

Small Change (1976)—A French film by François Truffaut that takes a look at a few small children with some free time on their hands who find their first loves. Sounds trite, but it isn't, and it also serves well to remind us of how we spent our summers when we were too young to go to the movies by ourselves.

The Sure Thing (1985)—A very likable film about two college students (John Cusack and Daphne Zuniga) who share a ride across the country for spring break (she to meet her boyfriend and he to meet his "sure thing"). Of course, after they hate each for a while, they start to, well, you know. No surprises, but quite enjoyable mainly due to the acting.

Valley Girl (1983)— A very 1980s film starring Nicholas Cage as a skate-rat Valley punker, who falls in love with a valley girl and proceeds to romance her in his own awkward way. A lot of fun and a completely different look at summer in California.

Mystic Pizza (1988)—Love and pizza among the locals and summer visitors of a small, Connecticut town. Four young friends work together at a local parlor and help each other through young love and the heartbreak of summer romance.

MUSIC

If you spent your entire summer watching MTV or VH1 (which we think would be a really bad idea), you would hear very little new or exciting music. Why not take some time this summer to experiment? Listen to some jazz, classical, early blues, or world music. If your parents have some dusty LPs or strange CDs, go through them. They almost certainly have some cool stuff.

Guess Where You'll Find It?

Unfortunately, it's nearly impossible to rent music from stores, but you'll be able to find some selections at the library. Libraries usually keep a collection of CDs, records, and cassettes. Try out some opera or some early jazz. Listen to the music a few times and try to get acquainted with what is going on before you give up on anything.

Just as you should keep a journal of the movies you see, try to write something on any new music that you've heard. By doing so, you'll find that you can get something from music that even your parents think is old-fashioned.

And while you're listening, try to find out something about the culture surrounding the music. If the music was composed by Johann Bach, a great German composer, spend some time learning about him. If it's by Sid Vicious, one of the fathers of punk, find out what his deal was, and maybe rent the movie *Sid and Nancy* to get an idea of his outrageously self-destructive lifestyle.

Saturday Night—Live!

Even though it might be hard to convince your parents, summer is the perfect time to see concerts. There's nothing like a live show. When thousands of people are all screaming in unison, a song can take a new significance.

You also might want to keep you eyes peeled for local performances. Lots of towns and cities have a cheap (or even free!) summer concert series. You can find everything from chamber music to flamenco. Often, these shows are given outdoors. Round up some friends, grab a blanket and some food, and spread out on the grass. It's a guaranteed good time.

 Moira Kiltie of Ridgewood, New Jersey was a self-professed Deadhead during her high school years. Once she got her driver's license at seventeen, she and her friends would take long trips to watch the Grateful Dead perform in different cities: "I thought it was a growing experience. We were away from home. We were with a lot of different people from all over the country. There were folks from California and from Texas at the New Jersey shows. It was really cool. We had a lot of fun."

They spent more time planning their trips than actually taking them: "We'd find out when the Dead were going to be in our area. On one summer we followed them from Connecticut down to Maryland for a period of about two weeks. We sometimes did it more than once in a summer. We based our trips on the Dead schedule and how far we thought our parents would let us get away and how much money we had."

A Dead show was more than a rock concert: "We were making tie-dyes and jewelry, so in the afternoons people would head out to the parking lot. We always made sure we had enough food to share with people. Oftentimes when we were camping, we'd meet our neighbors and set up the camping stuff. It was kind of like a fair or a festival."

Although following a band for a few days can be a great experience, you have to be careful: "I can remember people getting in the wrong crowd, people that they might not have trusted in other situations. They were excited about where they were and had gotten dulled into thinking, 'Hey, we're all Deadheads.'"

She also advises that you keep your trip fairly short: "It's an excitable crowd. It's a big crowd. People haven't slept. You have to know when it's enough. I had about a ten-day limit. I couldn't deal with not being sure when I could shower or where I would be sleeping. We didn't use our parents' money; we always saved our own money for these things. If I couldn't afford it, I wouldn't have done it."

With festivals like Lollapalooza and other shows, there are plenty of opportunities to follow a band. Just keep your head and make sure you have planned ahead. Also, because summer is the popular time to see shows, you might find it hard to get tickets. Get tickets early for the more popular bands.

COUNTRY

Johnny Cash—At Folsom Prison
Cash's famous baritone live, for the inmates. Listen to them cheer after Cash sings, "I shot a man in Reno just to watch him die."

Loretta Lynn—Blue-Eyed Kentucky Girl
"When you're lookin' at me, you're lookin' at country"; Lynn's about as genuine as it gets—a real coal miner's daughter.

Willie Nelson and Waylon Jennings—(If I Can Find A) Clean Shirt
Country outlaws Willie and Waylon sing about what they know best: hard drinkin', mean women, fighting, bad luck, and doing the laundry.

Hank Williams—24 of Hank Williams' Greatest Hits
The honky-tonk legend. Even folks that hate country love Hank.

Doc Watson—The Essential Doc Watson
He's not a household name, but after you hear this album, you'll wonder why. He could teach Eddie Van Halen a few things about guitar, too.

Dolly Parton—Best There Is
Don't smirk. Just listen to Jolene and deal with that awesome voice.

Patsy Cline—Heartaches
When the one you love treats you like a little ball of snot, this is the album to sob by (but keep sharp objects out of reach).

Bill Monroe—Bluegrass Ramble
In Japan, Monroe would be declared a living cultural treasure. The man simply is bluegrass.

Clifton Chenier—King of the Bayous
Like Monroe, Chenier has defined his music: zydeco. Put on this CD and attempt not to dance, yell, and have a great ol' time. You will undoubtedly fail.

k d lang—Absolute Torch and Twang
The voice of the modern age telling us that real, good country music is not dead and buried. lang's beautiful, strong voice has made many a naysayer take a walk through the country section of the local record store.

CLASSICAL

Because there are literally thousands of recordings of most of these pieces, we're not recommencing specific CDs, just compositions we think you'll enjoy.

Bach—Toccata and Fugue; the Brandenburg Concertos
Toccata and Fugue features the scariest, hugest organ chord ever—really. The Brandenburg Concertos make you feel like you're the silver flash from the scales of a school of a million fish in the middle of a sun-drenched ocean or dancing naked on a tiny blue ice cube or . . . you know, like that.

Beethoven—The Symphonies
Mess up your hair and air-conduct to your heart's delight in the privacy of your own room.

Mozart—Don Giovanni; Requiem Mass for the Dead
The music of this child prodigy turned adult virtuoso lights up any stereo.

Shumann—Piano Concerto in A minor
In between bouts of raving madness, he wrote great music.

Chopin—Nocturnes
Gorgeous and melancholy melodies.

Mussorgsky—Pictures from an Exhibition
Beeg Russian Zymphony!!!

Copeland—Appalachian Spring
Copeland took West Virginia folk melodies and turned them into truly American classical music.

Mahler—First and Sixth Symphonies
Lushly and moodily dark. Put on Mahler, turn off the lights, and brood over why you were born. Then turn the lights back on and shake it off.

Karl Orff—Caramina Burana
Orff took medieval students' drinking songs and gave them a choral orchestral setting. The musical result is like going slowly mad in the locked chamber of a high stone tower overlooking the black sea. But in a good way.

Stravinsky—The Firebird Suite
Stravinsky's music outraged Paris. At some of his premieres the audience hurled insults, rotten fruit, and chairs. Great stuff for the misunderstood genius in us all.

JAZZ

Charlie Parker—The Quintet: Jazz at Massey Hall
The Bebop virtuoso plays what is essentially a toy saxophone (he'd hocked his good one) and gives an inspired performance with an illustrious back-up band (Dizzy Gillespie, Bud Powell, Charlie Mingus, and Max Roach). A truly legendary moment in jazz.

Miles Davis—Kind of Blue
The coolest of cool jazz. Davis's breathy, slow mystical trumpet playing at its finest.

Thelonius Monk—Mark's Music
One of the great musical weirdos of all time. Monk's jagged, rhythmically disturbed piano playing might confuse you at first, but give it a chance. It's so clean, so true.

John Coltrane—A Love Supreme
Speaking of strange genius, John Coltrane is another one. Coltrane asks God deep questions with his sax. And, yes, God speaks saxophone.

Charles Mingus—Ah Um
The bassist/composer extraordinaire's signature album.

Betty Carter—Feed the Fire
Power jazz vocals.

Bill Evans Trio—Waltz for Debbie
Just a beautiful album.

George Gershwin—Rhapsody in Blue
This widely recorded piece is sweet and bluesy. It could easily be put in the classical category but don't let that worry you. Gershwin's in a class by himself.

Dave Brubeck—Time Out
Brubeck set out to write tunes in unusual time signatures and ended up with a classic jazz album.

Duke Ellington—In a Mellotone
Ellington and his music are the essence of sophistication and savoir faire. If music could make you drunk, Ellington would be the finest champagne.

SUMMER

George Gershwin—Porgy and Bess

What, Gershwin again? This is the opera that features "Summertime . . . and the livin' is easy." By the way, the rest of the opera's pretty good too."

The Beach Boys—Endless Summer

The title says it all. Surf's up.

Billie Holiday—The Summer of '49

Ms. Holiday's soft, bluesy, heartbreaking crooning can cool the most fevered brow.

Parliament Funkadelic—Maggot Brain

Don't let the truly disgusting title keep you from the freakiest, funkiest band that ever slapped a bass and wore twenty-inch, high-heel glitter shoes.

Red Hot Chili Peppers—Blood, Sugar, Sex, Magic

Great album. Great sweaty, sexy, summer feel.

The Drifters—16 Greatest Hits

Features "Up on the Roof" and "Under the Boardwalk." It doesn't get much more summery. Play this CD and your parents might come in the room and sing along. We're sorry about that.

Jimmy Cliff—The Harder They Come Soundtrack

A great reggae album. Now that's summer.

Ennio Morricone—A Fistful of Film Music

Morricone wrote the music for the majority of Italian "spaghetti westerns." If you've seen an old Clint Eastwood movie, you've heard Morricone. It's the music of high noon, of vultures circling in the desert, of mysterious senoritas whirling in shadowy candlelight.

The Grateful Dead—Workingman's Dead

Relax. It's summer.

Get Down on It

Whether you rockin' with your friends to the Stones or tuning out the hassles with your walkman and the Breeders, here's some great music to check out.

ROCK

Pink Floyd—Wish You Were Here

On certain bizarrely sunny Thursdays, we believe this album is superior to the highly regarded and splendid Dark Side of the Moon. The opening track should be listened to in a dark room with your stereo's equalizer lights clearly visible.

David Bowie—Hunky Dory

Young, pre-glam Bowie. We feel you should acquire this album. Then, we feel, you should gradually acquire all of Bowie's 1970s albums. But that's just us.

Velvet Underground—VU

Someone said it's pleasurable to listen to VU because you can sing along with Lou Reed and not feel so bad. This person was clearly mad or aurally-challenged, because Lou Reed is one of the greatest vocalists who has ever lived.

Bob Dylan—Bringing It All Back Home

It's hard to recommend just one Dylan album, but we think this one is a good place to start. It's right at that post-folk moment in Dylan's career when his superstardom was fresh, his voice clear, and his lyrics/poems astonishing (especially on "Gates of Eden").

Rickie Lee Jones—Rickie Lee Jones

This is her first and most acclaimed album, and the reason you should own it is because she's one of the slickest women on the planet. Note her ability to scat.

Joni Mitchell—Blue

This is minimalist, jazzy, folksy, rock music accompanied by a remarkably versatile voice hitting clean notes.

Tom Waits—Rain Dogs

This album is not characteristic of Waits' early piano balladeer persona but addresses similar themes. It rocks considerably, as well. (Pointless trivia: ex-boyfriend of Rickie.)

The Rolling Stones—Exile on Main Street

They're the originals, the real thing—and no music collection is complete without at least one of their albums. We think this album will give you an inkling as to why they're still around. It's just got that great bluesy, folksy rock thing that made them so very cool.

The Breeders—Last Splash

This is one of the best sister acts you'll ever find. They're raucous, fun, and they stand out in the sea of bands that have popped up in recent years (no easy task). They're pretty great to see live, too.

Sharpen
Your Skills

MAKE TIME

While you definitely should be having as much fun as possible in June, July, and August, it also might not be a bad idea to learn how to do things you didn't have time to check out during the school year. There are certain skills that are possible for you to teach yourself over the summer. The trick is to work systematically and not to get discouraged. Start by setting yourself a schedule. Maybe even write it out on a piece of paper.

For example:

10:00 - 10:30	*wake up and eat breakfast*
10:30 - 1:00	*study computer program*
1:00 - 2:00	*eat lunch*
2:00 - 7:00	*work on project*

It's totally possible to budget your time so you can work a job (or complete a project), hang out with friends, and still have time to sharpen your skills for a few hours a day this summer.

Teach Yourself How to Use a Computer

If there's a computer in your house and you don't know how to use it, take some time this summer to learn some programs. If you don't have a computer, maybe you can find one at a friend's house or the library. We don't care what field you decide to study or what career you plan to enter; you'll be using a computer. Now is a good time to gain some proficiency.

Make Some Money with Your PC

In addition to learning word processing, you might want to teach yourself Pagemaker or Quark. These are page layout programs that are used to set type in books and newsletters. In combination with word processing, these programs may be what you need to get a summer job. If you get good at enough of them, you could even design and publish your own newspaper or magazine (which, incidentally, would be a great thing to discuss in your college essays).

Go Online

If you don't have a modem, get one. The possibilities are endless. You can explore the internet, join news groups, and keep in touch with computer penpals thousands of miles away. There are several different online possibilities, ranging from the big commercial services (Compuserve or America Online) to smaller services that give you direct access to the Net.

The internet is constantly changing, and by the time this is published, new services may have started up and old ones will be defunct. But the internet and online services are communication tools that can be used to "meet" new people. If you have some obscure interests that nobody else in your town shares, you'll have no trouble finding someone out there with a computer who shares that interest. The easiest way to find these people is in the Usenet groups. These are "locations" on the internet where people who share the same interests hang out. There are groups for TV shows, rock bands, sports teams, colleges, and anything else imaginable. If you really get into it, you can even start your own group.

And then there's the Web, probably the most fun and easy-to-use of the internet services. The World Wide Web is a series of documents that are linked to each other through "hypertext links." A page of the Web might contain highlighted words or pictures that connect to computers anywhere else on the system. If you're looking for an alternative to TV to while away your time, consider exploring the World Wide Web; you will learn something about the net, and maybe some other stuff on the way.

SAT PREP

Let's face it. SATs are important to your future. If you're going to start your junior year next fall, this summer is the perfect time to begin studying. Even if you will be a freshman or a sophomore next year, you can still spend the summer increasing your vocabulary in preparation for the SAT. For years and years, a rumor has circulated that the SAT is a measure of your intelligence. This simply is not true. We at the Princeton Review have had years of experience teaching high school students just like you how to increase their scores. Regardless of what anyone may have told you, the SAT is coachable, and this summer might be a perfect time to study for your SAT.

Prep Courses Actually Raise Scores

There are several ways to prepare for the SAT. Without a doubt, the most comprehensive instruction available is through a prep course. A good course will give you personal instruction from energetic and highly trained teachers. It will have small classes and one-on-one instruction. In addition, many of the summer programs listed in this book offer SAT prep classes. Taking an SAT course while at a summer program is a good way to increase your score.

Stretch Your Mouth

If you're not ready for an SAT prep course, you can still start studying with books like the Princeton Review's *Cracking the SAT*. There are many things that you can do even in ninth or tenth grade, like learning new vocabulary. The best way to do that is to read and look up each word you run across that you don't know. But you can also absorb vocabulary rapidly by studying words and their definitions systematically. If you work at it a little bit each day, you can improve your vocabulary dramatically over the summer.

If you'd like a shortcut to learning vocabulary, find yourself a list of words. We recommend *Word Smart* and *Word Smart II*, which contains the most frequently used difficult words in the English language. Then, set yourself a goal, say ten words a day (about 1,000 words for the summer), and begin studying. Make a set of flashcards with the day's words on them, and carry them around to test yourself. Try to use the words as much as you can. On the weekend, review the words that you learned that week. By the end of the summer, you could have increased the verbal part of your SAT score substantially.

Academic Programs

GETTING AHEAD

You might be sick of school and ready for a break, but before you decide that an academic program isn't for you, you should realize that the atmosphere at a summer program is much more relaxing than at regular school. Even if you get grades, they will not appear on your transcript. You can study things just because they interest you.

Many of the programs that we've included offer the same activities that camps do. The difference is that these programs focus on learning. If you go, you will not only have a good time, but you'll probably come back a little better prepared to deal with academics in the fall.

You will take classes and do homework and all the rest of the stuff you normally do in school, but there is a lot less pressure and you'll have freedom to study your interests.

PUBLIC SUMMER SCHOOL

Although you might think it torture to return to those classrooms you recently escaped, public summer school can be a good idea for your summer vacation. Most summer school programs are for remedial work. If you haven't passed enough math classes, for example, you might need to take one during summer school so you can graduate with your class. If you're having trouble in one area, summer school can help you improve. And if you feel like your grades in one area aren't up to snuff, think about taking a class when you won't have to concentrate on the rest of high school's distractions.

Summer School Isn't Just for Slackers

If you go to a public high school that offers college-level courses with certain pre-requisites, you can take summer school to get these out of the way. Let's say, for example, that you want to take AP biology in your junior year, but you need to have three years of high school science. By taking one of those classes over the summer, you'll be able to move into the advanced class. Of course, because the class will be abbreviated, you might not get as much out of it. But you can fulfill the requirement and take the AP course earlier.

Most of the time, a day at public summer school is shorter than a day of normal school, so you'll still be able to work or make plans with your friends during the day. Look at public summer school as a way to get some easy courses out of the way, so that you can take more challenging classes.

 Margaret LeMore of Orlando, Florida went to summer school in the summer after her freshman year of high school. While she didn't particularly enjoy the summer, it fulfilled a requirement: "It was just a means to an end. It allowed me to take calculus in high school. Because of the sequencing of the math requirements, I had to take geometry over the summer or I wouldn't get to the calculus level by the end of the high school. I figured geometry would be the easiest math class to take over the summer."

The class work was anything but challenging. "The class was so lame that this one kid kept falling asleep in class. The teacher decided to teach this kid a lesson. She said 'I think we should paint his nails.' So she took out some pink nail polish and started to paint his nails. She only got a couple done before he woke up. At that point, I knew just how little I was going to get out of summer school."

Even though the class wasn't challenging, LeMore felt she learned what she needed to: "I never felt at a disadvantage later on even though it had been such an easy class, so I must have learned something. We didn't have any homework. Most of the people in there really needed to pass, so the teacher wanted to guarantee that they did the work."

If you do go to summer school, LeMore suggests that you keep it in perspective: "Don't take it too seriously. Do other things during your summer so you don't feel like you wasted it."

Other Local Academic Options

Maybe you're satisfied with the education you're getting during the school year but are looking for something a little different over the summer. But private school is only for the kids that are already in the school, right? Well, actually, most private schools don't allow their students to attend summer courses — they aim to attract students from other places. If you live next to one of the private programs listed on the following pages, you can go as a day student.

THE PRINCETON REVIEW WAY OF FINDING A GOOD LOCAL SUMMER SCHOOL

First, speak to your high school counselor. She should be able to give you a list of summer schools in your area. Don't feel compelled to go to your own school's program (if it has one); you may find more interesting classes and meet new people somewhere else. Ask about local colleges in the area. Many of these take high school students and give them a chance to study college-level courses. Also, ask your counselor if she knows of other students who have done summer study. If so, find them and question them. Find out if they learned a lot and if they liked the teachers.

Second, once you get a list of programs that are available, call for a brochure or catalog; try to decide what type of courses and what level of difficulty you want. In general, the more competitive the admissions process is at a college, the harder the classes are, but if you have questions check out a good guide to colleges. If you're interested in a program, try to get the name of someone who attended. Call him and ask him: "Were the classes challenging?" "How big were the classes?" "How good was the instruction?"

Depending on where you live, you could have a lot of choices, but if you live in a small town, you may have to travel to find a good program. We have also listed in the following pages a group of excellent programs for people who want to live away from home over the summer.

PREP SCHOOL PROGRAMS

If you want a program that's academically enriching, has great instructors, and gives you the chance to live away from home, you should consider attending a prep school for the summer. These programs are sometimes hard to get into and tend to be a little expensive, but if you do get in, you'll be studying in a challenging environment with other intelligent students. The classes are generally excellent. They are taught by the same teachers that work at the prep schools during the school year. Plus, because prep schools are used to dealing with high school students, you'll have lots of great activities to choose from.

Although you won't be at an actual college campus, the programs that we list are at some of the most prestigious private schools in the country. Even if you go to public school, you can impress college admissions staff with your work at one of these programs. If you do want to attend a program at a college campus, we've listed the best on-campus programs we could find on pages 143-154.

These prep schools are generally more academically oriented than the on-campus programs we list. The classes are challenging, and you'll have lots of homework to do. This is not to say, however, that the programs aren't fun. The people running the program have years and years of experience working with high school students, and they know how to set up an environment that is conducive to learning and yet allows you some free time.

The Phillips Academy Summer Session (Andover)

Address 180 Main Street, Andover, MA 01810-4166

Phone (508) 749-4400

Fax (508) 749-4414

Cost $3,350 (Approximately 15 percent of the students are on financial aid. Interested applicants should apply regardless of their income. Financial aid deadline is March 1. No financial aid given to international students.)

Ages 14–18

Class size About 14 students

Size of program 660 students

Length of program 42 days

Application deadline Early applications are preferred. All applications are processed in the order in which they are received.

Description Summer academic program at a prep school.

Summary A challenging academic program for good students looking for small classes and excellent instruction.

History As the oldest boarding school in the nation, Phillips Academy, Andover has a strong commitment to teaching some of the best students in the nation. This place is steeped in history, and your stay there will connect you to students from the two centuries of the prep school's history. This is where

George Washington sent his nephews, Paul Revere engraved the school's seal, and Samuel Smith penned *America*. In the summer program, Phillips Academy gives an experience to kids who would not normally get the chance.

The Program First and foremost, Andover is an academic program. The classes are hard with lots of homework, but if you're willing to work, you will succeed. Classes are small with both teachers and teaching assistants in the classes. The teachers go deeper into a subject than you might expect, and they expect you to work at a quick pace to keep up.

The facilities are amazing. A huge library, an art gallery, a museum of archaeology, a computer center, a writing center, a language laboratory, a music library, and a nature sanctuary are all on the 450 acre, beautifully landscaped campus. Andover's fine arts programs are one of its strengths. Due to the recent construction of the Elson art center on campus, arts students can work with state-of-the-art facilities to produce their work.

In addition, Andover has a program called OCEANS in which students study marine biology and oceanography on land and at sea. Ten days of the program are spent on a 55-foot ship sailing the seas around Cape Cod where the students research the marine environment and the humpback whale.

If you are willing to study hard and have a desire to learn in a diverse student body, Andover is a great program. Its small classes and inspiring teachers ensure that you'll learn a lot.

 Jennifer Corman, a public school student from Niskayuna, New York studied at Andover the summer before her senior year. She was impressed with the program and its teachers: "I loved it. It was wonderful. It was really personalized. I had classes with only fifteen people, and the teachers took an active interest in the students and were always available to help. For my anatomy class (my major), both the TA and the teacher had a review session the night before the exam. They went over the stuff for the exam. If we had a problem, we could see them for help. They were really responsive to our questions and our requests for help. The classes were very hard. There was a lot of work. For my major, there was an average of three to four hours of homework a night. Everyone did it. We complained, but we knew we wanted to be at Andover."

The living conditions were unbelievable: "My dorm was great. I had one roommate and we had three rooms. It was huge, we had plenty of room. My roommate and I kind of lucked out."

While an Andover program isn't for everyone, it is for "anybody who's willing to do the work and is also willing to meet new people and really have a different experience. There's a lot of work at my school at home, but I was really shocked. After the first day, I had like three hours of homework."

If you do go to the program, Corman advises that you "be outgoing the first couple of weeks and try to meet a lot of people. Keep in step with your homework, don't let it all pile up the night before it's due."

Choate Rosemary Hall

Address P.O. Box 788, Wallingford, CT 06492-0788

Phone (203) 697-2365

Fax (203) 697-2519

E-mail Nancy Miller@QM.CHOATE.EDU

Cost $3,200 (Financial aid is available based on financial need. Apply early to receive it.)

Ages 13–18

Class size 12, with an instructor and an intern

Size of program 478 students

Length of program 34 days

Application deadline Spring, but early applications ensure first choice of classes.

Description Summer academic program at a prep school.

Summary A challenging academic program for good students looking for excellent instruction.

History Formed through the merger of two 100-year-old prep schools, Choate Rosemary has hosted a summer program since 1916. They believe that small, challenging classes in a supportive environment can help high school students achieve their potential. The program combines challenging academics with a beautiful campus and lots of fun.

The Program If you go to Choate Rosemary Hall over the summer, expect to work. They estimate that the average student will have three hours of homework a night, which means you'll be learning a lot. The classes are small and there's nowhere to hide, so slacking off is no easy task. But somehow, most students seem to find a way to socialize.

Courses are available in almost anything. There are courses in fine arts, music, computer science, English, history, social sciences, languages, mathematics, physical education, psychology, philosophy, and science. Each day you will take two major (80 minute) courses and one minor (either forty minutes and homework or eighty minutes with no homework). Many of the teachers are from the Choate Rosemary Hall prep school, and some are public school teachers from the area who have been teaching at the program for years.

The facilities are impressive. The school has all kinds of computers and a beautiful campus. Four days a week, you have to participate in athletics or community service, and you'll have plenty of choices for athletics, with the usual assortment of tennis, soccer, swimming, and basketball plus some more specialized skills like karate and yoga. Weekend excursions are planned. You can go to Boston, New York City, a Yankees game, and more.

Choate Rosemary has several special programs as well. They have an English Language institute for non-native English speakers, The John F. Kennedy Institute in Government, which focuses on the political process, and The Writing Project, which allows students to focus on their writing. In addition, Choate Rosemary offers a summer in Paris and Spain.

Choate Rosemary Hall's summer program is a great way to expand your mind and take challenging courses. If you go to public school now, you will be impressed with the small classes and excellent facilities. Admission is fairly competitive, so if you like to learn among good students, this is the place for you.

 Mimi Kelly of Connecticut went to Choate Rosemary Hall's summer program the year before her senior year. She was really impressed: "I had the best time. It was so great. I met people from all over the world. I live in a not very diverse place. It was just amazing. I went in with stereotypes, and when I came out and they were totally gone. I made some of the best friends in five weeks that I think I've ever had."

She was really impressed with the academics: "I go to public school in honors and AP classes and the classes were about equal in difficulty. The one class was Political Ideologies, and we had to write two papers, we had quizzes every week, a big midterm, and a final. For one week, we had a mock election. We worked in pairs to set up a candidate. On Friday, we all got together and presented our platform. The class was well taught. I'm into history, and it was really interesting. The teachers were very nice. They really cared about the kids a lot, and the student interns were great too. Some kids took SAT prep classes and some came to prepare for their classes next year. I went for enrichment purposes. There were no more history classes in my school, and I wanted to learn more."

If you do go to Choate Rosemary Hall, Kelly recommends that you, "be as outgoing as possible. It's a warm atmosphere. Everyone I met wanted to be there. Do as much as you can. Get involved as much as you can, too because it goes by so fast. The more you do, the more you have to remember later."

Cushing Academy

Address School St., Ashburnham, MA 01430-8000

Phone (508) 827-5911

Fax (508) 827-6927

Cost $3,950

Ages 10–18

Class size 10–12 students

Size of Program 420 students

Length of program 42 days

Application deadline Early applications are preferred. All applications are processed in the order in which they are received.

Description Summer academic program at a prep school.

Summary A challenging academic program for good students looking for a chance to excel.

History A boarding school for grades nine through twelve established in 1865, Cushing Academy offers students a chance to study in an academically challenging and also nurturing environment. Cushing Academy makes the most of its international student body, offering many opportunities to meet new people from all over the world.

The Program Cushing Academy is an academic experience. The small classes are challenging with lots of homework, but if you do work hard, you'll learn a lot and still have some free time. One of the more exciting programs is their critical language program

which allows you to study a language intensively in the United States and still be able to converse with native speaking kids. The languages offered are ones that you will most likely not be able to take in school—Arabic, Chinese, Japanese, Korean, and Russian—and you'll be able to practice your skills with some of the international students attending. Roughly two-thirds of the students are from foreign countries, so you will get the experience of meeting all kinds of people while you are learning.

Cushing Academy also offers a critical skills program, which is great if you're having problems getting the grades you want. The classes are small (ten or twelve people), and you'll get a lot of individual instruction. The teachers will teach you the study skills you need to succeed in high school. Cushing Academy offers an excellent opportunity to further your academic goals.

The emphasis on academics doesn't mean that you'll be living a monk's life, however. There are plenty of things to get involved in. Each week, there are dances, sporting events, and musical performances. On weekends, you can travel to nearby Boston, and every Wednesday, you can go on a variety of field trips. Cushing Academy also recently opened an ice-skating facility. With professional instructors in both figure skating and hockey, you can increase your skills while learning at a first-class academic institution.

 Ben Kornitzer of Newton, Massachusetts went to Cushing Academy the summer before his senior year. He was impressed with the students and the quality of the program: "I thinks it's a very good program. It's very diverse. There are students from all over the world. Just on my floor in the dorm, you could go door to door and find no one from the same country or state."

He felt the program was well run: "All the programs brought the kids together. They did a lot of activities to bring a sense of school unity. In the middle of the program, we had a summer fling, which was a carnival out on the football fields. There were obstacle courses and a bungee run. You're strapped to a bungee cord. You ran as far as you could, and you bounced off these padded walls. It was a lot of fun."

Although the program had a lot of fun things to do, there was also plenty of work: "I'm from a fairly challenging public school. I think the course work here is pretty intense. But even though you are

covering a lot of material, the teachers make it fairly relaxed. There are breaks, and these make it easier. I had about two hours of homework a night. They're very understanding of your schedule. If there's going to be a big school event the next day, they'll taper off the homework.

"The small classes were great. The first thing our chemistry teacher did was give us his phone number. He said to call any time. We have supervised study every single night, and if a student was having trouble, our teacher gave him two hours of extra help every day. It was almost like you had a private tutor."

Kornitzer especially remembers "International Night," which happened once a week during dinner: "They totally transform the dining hall. Every nationality sets up its own booth. The food is fantastic. Probably around twenty-five countries are represented. You go to one booth and have tempura, you go to another and get crepes. All the students wear their traditional garb. Some Arabic kids wore flowing white robes, some Asian kids wore kimonos."

If you do go on the program, Kornitzer has the following advice: "Go in there with a really open mind about the different cultures you'll meet. They offer so much here. If you're not doing a full-time sport, you can do an elective at night. They have a choir and a band. They have sports tournaments all the time. Take advantage of everything. Don't be afraid to try something new."

Phillips Exeter Academy Summer School

Address 20 Main St., Exeter, NH 03833-2460

Phone (800) 828-4325, ext. 3488; (603) 778-3488

Fax (603) 778-4385

E-mail peasummer@aol.com

Cost $3,300

Ages 13–18

Class size under 12

Size of program 545 students

Length of program 42 days

Application deadline Early applications are preferred. Applications are processed in the order in which they are received.

Description An academic enrichment program at a prep school.

Summary A challenging and well-rounded program for students wishing to push themselves academically and physically. Has a fairly diverse and international student body.

History Since 1919, the Exeter summer school has been challenging students. They believe that students should learn for the sheer

pleasure of it, and they have made every effort to ensure that a multicultural student body attends the school.

The Program Although it offers excellent physical education and enjoyable excursions, Exeter is at heart an academic program. Through its faculty and small classes (usually under twelve), Exeter offers an incredible educational experience for students willing to work hard and push themselves.

The range of subjects available is truly outstanding. Because of its relatively large size, Exeter can offer classes in a lot of areas. Students take three courses that meet five times a week. Courses are available in English, history, humanities, foreign languages, math, computer science, music, performing arts, psychology, and science.

The music instruction at the school is excellent. Exeter offers musicians a chance to learn their craft while studying a well-rounded curriculum. In addition, Exeter makes good use of its remarkably diverse student body. People are encouraged to show off their talents and their culture, and in the weekly assembly program, students can perform arts from their home countries.

Exeter also has a range of excursions planned for the weekends. You can go to Boston and see museums, the aquariums, and more. If you want a summer school in a challenging environment with other smart students, Exeter is the place for you.

Monty Hobson of St. Louis, Missouri went to Exeter Academy the summer before his sophomore year of high school. He felt the program was great: "The teaching was unbelievable. The instructors use the Harkness plan, in which a maximum of 12 students sit at a circular table with chairs all the way around. It gives the teacher a better feel for the class.

"I took advanced algebra, creative writing, and architecture. I go to public school, but the classes were still doable. There weren't that many classes in the day, so I wouldn't call it too difficult. It's work, but there's a lot of free time, too. There's school in the day, fun in the afternoon, and work at night. It's a good balance."

Hobson especially remembers the time he was the lead in the play. "I got into the second act of Our Town and I froze. I basically forgot my line. The funny thing is I stayed on stage. I ended up skipping an entire scene. What was neat about that was that the entire cast covered for me. I said the wrong line, the actors backstage came out on that wrong line, and the audience almost didn't know the difference. It could have been a disaster, but we just stuck together."

He felt that the program was good for all types of people: "I think that the truth of the matter is that it doesn't take anyone special. Even someone who doesn't think they'll like it will. It didn't fit anyone's personality, all types go. From preppy to punk to skater. I didn't meet anyone who thought that the program was whack."

If you do go, Hobson advises that you "don't go in expecting anything. Go in as if you know nothing about it. Let the program come to you instead of trying to tackle it. You'll find that if your expectations are way too high, you might be disappointed. I mean it's school. It's not summer camp. If you don't want to be stressed out, this isn't the place to come. It's school, but it's a good school."

Northfield Mount Hermon Summer School

Address 206 Main St., Northfield, MA 01360

Phone (413) 498-3290

Fax (413) 498-3112

Cost $3,450 (Financial aid is available based on financial need. Interested applicants should apply regardless of their income.)

Ages 11–18

Class Size averages 10

Size of program 460 students

Length of program 42 days

Application deadline Early applications are preferred. Applications are processed in the order in which they are received.

Description An academic enrichment program at a prep school

Summary A challenging and well-rounded program for students wishing to push themselves academically. Has a fairly diverse and international student body.

History Northfield Mount Hermon School provides a challenging academic program for students looking to focus in one area. With excellent instructors drawn primarily from the boarding school's regular teaching staff, the school offers you an opportunity to excel and learn at a rapid rate.

The Program Northfield Mount Hermon school is primarily an academic enrichment program. This means that you will have challenging classes with lots of homework. The courses are structured so that you get a full year of high school course work in one six-week session. In addition, the small classes ensure that you'll get lots of one-on-one teaching and that you'll be asked to participate.

In addition to the academics, you'll spend your afternoons relaxing or competing in sporting events. The campus is beautiful with incredible facilities, and a large number of international students attend. This means you can meet people from all over the world while studying at a first-rate institution.

Besides the traditional academic subjects offered at most high schools, Northfield Mount Hermon also offers critical language study in Japanese or Arabic. This program offers language instruction with the following summer spent in Japan or Egypt. In addition, this year the school is offering a college explorations session where you'll learn about how to get into college and about the different colleges out there.

Catherine Keyser, of Seagirt, New Jersey studied at Northfield Mount Hermon the summer before her junior year. She was impressed: "It was just wonderful. The six weeks made it feel like you were going to totally live there for the rest of your life. As soon as you get there, you just feel like you're a part of it."

Keyser normally attends a mediocre public school. She found the difference between her school and Northfield Mount Hermon was huge: "It's like heaven compared to public school. It's like you landed where academics are supposed to be. First of all, the classes aren't enormous like at most public schools, and second of all, all the teachers are there cause they want to be. They're completely enthusiastic and completely receptive to you as an individual. For the whole six weeks, I was just pinching myself asking, 'Am I really here?' It was like a breath of fresh air. I made such good friends."

She was really impressed with her classes: "The classes were fabulous. I just loved my creative writing class. The workshop was really valuable. The entire class looked at your work and give a critique of it. You didn't only have the teacher and the teacher fellow looking at the work, but you had all the kids in the class looking at your work and that was terrific."

She especially remembers one rainy Sunday afternoon: "My roommate and a friend of ours were all sitting in our room and just talking. All of a sudden it started to rain, and I had this urge to go outside and run in the rain. So I turn to my friends and asked, 'Do you want to go outside?' Without saying another word, all three of us ran outside as fast as we could and we danced in the rain for about fifteen minutes. It was great."

If you do go, Keyser advises that you should be "completely yourself. A lot of times kids stifle a part of themselves when they are in school. At Northfield, there is always someone who'll be able to appreciate you. Everyone I met was incredible. It will be one of the greatest summers you'll ever have. Take advantage of it to the fullest."

Summer at Taft

Address 110 Woodbury Rd., Watertown, CT 06795

Phone (203) 274-2516, ext. 243

Fax (203) 945-3110

Cost $3,400

Ages 12–17

Class size Averages 8

Size of program 160

Length of program 35 days

Application deadline Early applications are preferred. Applications are processed in the order in which they are received.

Description An academic enrichment program at a prep school

Summary An excellent opportunity to take challenging academic classes taught by great teachers. Taft's small size ensures that you'll be treated as an individual.

History The Taft school was established in 1890 by President William Howard Taft's brother. Through its small classes and limited enrollment, Taft makes the summer school an exciting place to learn. The school's motto— "Not to be served, but to serve"— is an accurate representation of its teaching philosophy. They expect you to take an active part in the learning process.

The Program Summer at Taft is primarily an academic program. You'll be spending thirty hours a week in class, and each class will give you a good deal of homework. The courses make up the backbone of a traditional liberal arts education, with offerings in English, mathematics, science, languages, history, and the arts. In addition, there are courses in computers and SAT preparation.

Taft's small size is one of its strengths. You will get to know the faculty, and they will get to know you. With classes as small as three students a piece, you will get a huge amount of one-on-one instruction. If you're attending public school now, this can be a breath of fresh air. The teachers will want to hear your opinion and will encourage discussion. If you don't do your work, the teacher will know about it.

Besides academics, Taft also requires that you participate in athletics or volunteer work for one hour and fifteen minutes each day in the afternoon. The facilities are fantastic, with tennis courts, playing fields, and an eighteen-hole golf course. This can be a great chance to have fun and keep in shape.

If you're looking for an intimate summer school with great academics and small classes, take a look at Taft. It offers a good balance between academics and fun, and it will allow you to learn in a supportive environment.

 Ben Serillo, of New York, New York studied at Taft the summer before his sophomore year: "I thought it was a lot of fun. It's interesting to meet people from different parts of the country and world. The classes were thought out and well formulated. The teachers were very nice and professional."

The classes were challenging with about two hours of homework each day, but there was still plenty of time for fun. Serillo played sports: "We could choose each week what sport we wanted for the next week. I did two weeks of basketball, one week of soccer, football, and volleyball." And he met all kinds of people: "It was nice to meet some foreign people. I made friends with people from all over the world."

They went on several excursions. Serillo chose to go back to Manhattan: "I came back to Manhattan twice, once to a Met game and once to walk around the West Side. We went to the Museum of

Natural History, and for some reason everyone wanted to go to McDonald's. So the advisors walked with us to the McDonald's thirty blocks away."

If you do go to Taft, Serillo advises that you should relax: "Don't worry, it's just summer school. I was too uptight for it. I should have loosened up."

SUMMER ON-CAMPUS

Itching to go to college? One of the many options for the summer of 1996 is an on-campus program. These programs put you on a college campus and give you a taste of the college experience. Have you ever wondered what college will be like? Do you crave the on-campus atmosphere? Then these programs are for you.

But, first, let's define what we mean by an on-campus program. These are basically camps that are run from college campuses. You go through an abbreviated college semester with classes and other activities and get some of the activities and travel that you might find in other programs. Most of these programs include travel to local areas on the weekends, so you can get the experience of traveling and studying all from one program.

Is It for You?

These programs give you plenty of time to do your own thing. This can be a good and a bad thing. Not only will you be independent, but you will have to be responsible with your time. Most programs have an itinerary as follows:

You will spend the morning and afternoon in classes, and, from three until lights-out, you will be responsible for choosing your own activities. The better programs will give you some choice, but even the best still expect you to fend for yourself a lot of the time.

We have seen students thrive in this situation—studying for their courses or exploring the college town—but others find the situation unbearable and may leave the program feeling as if they have been bored the whole time. Just like in college, some people adapt quickly to the freedom, while others fool around, party too much, and don't finish their semesters. If you're not a self-starter and are unable to find things to do with your time, these programs may not be for you.

The Truth About Credit

Some of these programs offer college credit for attending and completing classes. This suggests that by finishing the program, you might be able to graduate from college in less time and save some money. While this is a nice idea in theory, many colleges don't accept these credits.

This does not mean that the courses have no practical value. Aside from the important stuff that you'll learn, some colleges accept the courses for advance placement, allowing you to skip out of some of the boring, first-year requirements. This can be a huge bonus. It's a good idea to call the college that you plan on attending and check to see if they accept the credits from a summer on-campus program.

But Maybe the Credit Isn't So Important Anyway

You'll have to ask yourself if you really want these credits. Do you want to graduate from college in fewer than four years? Most people find that they like college and that graduating early is not such a huge bonus anyway. So the lesson from all this is simple: Don't choose a program on its ability to offer you credit. Look for other, more important issues.

WHAT TO LOOK FOR IN AN ON-CAMPUS PROGRAM

Just like any of the summer programs, each on-campus program is different. Some give you small, specially designed classes for high school students, others will throw you in Psych 101. You have to decide what you feel is important. So here are some questions to ask:

How Big Are the Classes?

Of course, the best way to learn is in small classes. You won't get lost in the crowd, and you will be asked your opinion from time to time. So if you really want to learn in an interactive environment, make sure you find small classes. If, however, you want to experience what the first year of college is really going to be like, go for the big classes. Even at most small liberal arts colleges, your first year will have its share of large lectures. Large classes are a challenge, and a summer spent as a student number can be instructive. You have to take responsibility for your education and force yourself to concentrate on a professor 100 feet away. If you can learn to get something out of large lecture classes, you will do very well in your first year of school.

But the choice is really up to you. If you want to be in the thick of things, solving problems, and dealing directly with the teacher, try the small classes. If you want to experience what your first year in college might be like, go with the big ones.

Who Teaches the Classes?

Some programs offer classes taught by a combination of high school teachers, graduate students, and college professors. Obviously, who the teachers are isn't as important as how well they teach, but you should definitely take this information into consideration. Most freshman classes at large universities are partially taught by graduate teaching assistants. Although you might have a professor giving a weekly lecture, some of your class time will be led by an inexperienced graduate assistant. This can be good because you can learn what college is like by asking your teachers. Also, don't shy away from programs that use high school teachers. They know how to teach high school students and will help keep the classes interesting and fun.

What Is Planned for the Evenings?

As we said before, many of these programs have classes in the morning and afternoon and then leave you to your own devices in the evenings. Some of them have planned activities that you can choose to participate in. Find out what these are. Some may have no activities planned, and you will have to set up your own. If you're someone who is able to plan your time, then not having activities might not be such a bad thing, but if you worry about being bored, look for a program with lots to do.

What Is the Area Around the College Like?

Some campuses are in big cities with many activities. If you think you'll want to go to a movie or a museum, you should probably choose a program with its location in mind. Some campuses are fairly isolated, and you will be forced to do only the activities that are available on campus. If the campus is isolated, and there aren't too many planned activities, it could be a boring trip.

What Is Planned for the Weekends?

Many of these programs have weekend travel trips as a bonus (sometimes at an additional charge). Check out where they are going and see if it interests you. Find out how they are planning to get there. Are you expected to find your own way? Weekend trips can be a great time to get to know the other students at the program.

ON-CAMPUS PROGRAMS

The following programs are some of the best of the pre-college programs. They are run by independent companies, not the colleges, and have a reputation for great service. We feel we have a pretty good range here, from the Big Ten spirit of Penn State, to the more academically challenging ASA program at the University of Massachusetts/Amherst. In most of these programs, you'll have plenty of options when you're not in class. You'll be able to hang out, go on trips, visit other colleges, or play organized sports. They all have excellent counselors/residence advisors who will help you adjust to the college experience. In addition to offering courses in academic subjects, most of these programs offer excellent test-preparation classes as well.

To choose among them, you should first decide what kind of on-campus atmosphere you're looking for. All of the programs capture some of the flair of life on their host campuses. If you go to one at UCLA, you'll get a glimpse into life at a big state university. If you go to one at Williams, you'll see what life is like at a small northeastern school. You should also call up any program that you're interested in and order the brochure, which will tell you what courses are offered and what options are offered. To order, just call the toll-free number provided. In general, these programs' fees cover most everything you might want to do there. However, they all recommend bringing extra spending money, and some have special programs that cost a little extra.

Academic Studies Associates

Address 355 Main Street, P.O. Box 800, Armonk, NY 10504-0800

Phone (800) 752-2250; (914) 273-2250

Fax (914) 273-5430

E-mail 75471.2026@compuserve.com

Cost $2,395–$4,595

Ages 14–18

Class Size Most have fewer than 12 students

Size of programs 140–300 students

Length of program 21–42 days

Application Deadline Early applications are preferred. All are processed in the order in which they are received.

Description Pre-college enrichment programs in University of Massachusetts/Amherst, University of Colorado/Boulder, Stanford University, and Oxford University.

Summary A great introduction to life at college. Has small classes and great instructors. Offers exciting excursions to interesting places.

Special Options The Princeton Review SAT preparation $165–$400; Nick Bolliteri Tennis (at Amherst) $295–$495; Golf elective (at Amherst) $295–$495; Various excursions $40–$495.

History Since 1983, ASA has been running enrichment programs for high school students.

They believe that a pre-college program should be a good place to learn new things and to learn what it's like to be a college student. A person who goes to one of these programs will leave better able to handle the change from high school to college.

The Program ASA offers similar programs at the different campuses; differences are mostly due to location. If you go to Colorado, for example, you can learn how to rock climb or white-water raft; if you go to Amherst, you can visit Boston. We're going to describe the Stanford program, but we believe that you can get a pretty good sense of how all of their programs are set up.

You'll stay in the Stanford dorms on campus. The dorms are coed with single-sex floors, and each floor will have a resident advisor, a staff member from the program who will help you get the most from the experience. In the mornings on Monday through Friday, you'll spend three hours studying your major. There are majors in SAT prep, studio art, creative writing, modern physics, psychology, business, law, film, and more. The teachers will do everything to make the courses interesting and, because you'll be in small classes, you will be required to take part in discussion. The early afternoons will be spent on an elective, which can be any of the above courses, plus tennis. You will get a grade in your major, but the classes are really good.

Learning in a group of twelve people for three hours at a time is a lot different from your typical high school class. You'll be able to participate in discussions and explore areas that interest you.

From 3:15-5:30, you'll be able to choose from a laundry list of activities. You could work on the yearbook or literary magazine, experiment with improv theater, join the debate club, you could just go out and enjoy the sunny weather and play volleyball or tennis. After dinner, it's again up to you to decide what to do. You could attend a guest lecture or see a comedian. You could see a movie or play miniature golf. As you can tell, there will be a large number of activities to choose from.

The program aims to combine learning and fun. The homework load is fairly light, so you'll have plenty of time to experience college living and meet new friends. An ASA program is as much a social experience as a learning experience. You'll get a chance to live the college student life and learn at the same time.

The weekends offer a series of planned excursions to San Francisco, Yosemite National Park, and Los Angeles, so even though the program will be geared toward academics, you'll still have time to explore some of California. Most students leave the program with a much better sense of how they will react to the college experience. You will also develop strategies for making good use of your college years.

 Jonathan Volk of Portland, Maine went on the ASA pre-college program at Stanford. He was impressed: "I really, really enjoyed the program. It was wonderful. I've been on several programs, and the kids I met on this program were great. A lot of us had similar interests, and we were all there to gain something. We all really wanted to be there."

He felt like he got a good sense of Stanford University: "During the program I felt like I got a really good feel for the Stanford campus and the school." He was also greatly impressed with the teachers: "One of my teachers was a lecturer at Stanford, and the other got her M.A. from Stanford. What was neat was that they were young, and it was like being taught by our peers. Also, you could find some of the teachers outside of the classroom. One of my teachers was more than just a teacher. She was a teacher/friend/therapist. She was there to help students with their problems and not just to teach you an academic subject."

He felt that the excursions gave him a good sense of the area: "The excursions are one of the better parts of the program. You get a chance to get a really good feel for the area. We spent three days in San Francisco, and we got time on our own to walk around and explore— to get the feel for it."

His most memorable moment was on the last day of class: "When most of the kids were packing, a teacher came up to us and said, 'You can either pack or come with me. We're going fountain hopping. Go get your bathing suits.' There are four good-size fountains on campus. We ran to the first fountain and swam and splashed all the people walking by. We ran through campus in our bathing suits and splashed in the fountains one by one for about two hours."

Volk was also impressed by how well the program applied to everyone: "There was a big range of what kids wanted to get out of the program; some were there just to hang out, some were there to study hard and improve their SAT scores, but most of us wanted to socialize and meet new people and do some good work in the process. The majority of the program is the socializing and meeting new people. The work was as challenging as you wanted it to be."

If you do go on an ASA program, Volk advises that you "try to do as many of the activities that they offer as possible, including the excursions. That's where I met the most people and had the most fun— during the afternoon activities. Get involved."

Excel at Williams or Amherst

Address Putney, VT 05346

Phone (802) 387-5885

Fax (802) 387-4276

Cost $2,795–$3,795 (Limited financial aid is available based on need.)

Ages 14–19

Class Size 10–12 students per class

Size of program 150 students per session

Length of program 21–35 days

Application Deadline Early applications are preferred. Applications are processed in the order in which they are received.

Description On-campus programs at Williams and Amherst colleges.

Summary An introduction to college life with excellent courses and staff. Includes on-campus weekends and excursions.

Special Options The Princeton Review SAT preparation $380.

Sports clinics soccer $95; tennis $195; golf $195

Various excursion Ontario $240; Quebec $240; Montreal $165

History Founded in 1952, Putney Student Travel offers a range of programs for high school students. Their pre-college programs offer a combination of challenging courses

with a knowledgeable staff that makes for an exciting learning and growing opportunity. Putney believes that a more intimate program allows for individual instruction and lends to an experience that will be remembered for the rest of your life.

The Program Both Excel programs offer a good mix of learning and fun, and both will give you a good sense of what it's like to live and study on a college campus. Your instructors will stay with you and provide you with individual instruction. In addition to academics, Excel offers special instruction in athletics, the arts, and SAT preparation.

The choice of courses is truly impressive. With offerings in all fields, you'll definitely find something to interest you. From art to theater to ethics to field biology, they will have a course that interests you. Since the classes are small, you'll be forced to participate in discussions and will get individual instruction.

A typical day at one of these programs goes as follows. You'll begin with breakfast and then a morning seminar from 9:30-11:30. Then you have lunch, followed by more instruction. In the afternoons you can do a number of optional activities, from community service to private musical instruction. In the evenings are planned activities in which you can either participate or not.

Most weekends offer some type of travel or event. You might go white-water rafting or play golf or go mountain biking at Mount Snow. Trips to Manchester, Vermont, or Boston are also organized. In addition, there's one excursion planned for a long weekend in the middle of July, that will take you to one of four cities to explore.

An Excel program is a good chance to learn, play sports, and grow. You'll get to experience life on a college campus and to travel to exciting cities as well.

John Strasenburgh, a senior from Hanover, New Hampshire, studied with Excel at Williams College. Each student gets two courses at the program. He took the optional Princeton Review course in the morning and he took a photography course because he didn't want to get burned out. "The Princeton course was fairly intense, requiring homework everyday, but it paid off in the end." Strasenburgh's SAT scores shot up, and he is now planning to apply to better colleges than he would have before the program. He was especially impressed with the teachers: "I enjoyed the faculty. They were young and it was easy to relate to them."

Just like most on-campus programs, the classes end in the early afternoon, at which point you're on your own. Strasenburgh spent the afternoons relaxing: "I usually hung out with my friends or hung out playing hackeysack outside." And on the weekends, there are planned activities: "I went on a few fly-fishing trips on the Deerfield River. I did a lot of mountain biking in the area."

One of the best parts of the program was being on a college campus: "Being on the Williams Campus gave you a good sense of what college is like. You're finally realizing this is the real world." But to get the most out of it, you have to work hard: "A lot of people were slacking off, but some were working. I put my time in. While you're there, you might as well work. You can have a good time and meet a lot of people. But even if you don't enjoy it, if you work, you'll get something out of it."

Exploration at Wellesley College

Address 470 Washington Street, P.O. Box 368, Norwood, MA 02062

Phone (617) 762-7400

Fax (617) 762-7425

Cost $2,285–$4,270 (Scholarship program for inner-city Boston students)

Ages 12–18

Class Size Fewer than 15 students.

Size of program 500 students per session

Length of expedition 21–42 days

Application Deadline Early applications are preferred. Applications are processed in the order in which they are received.

Description An on-campus program at Wellesley College

Summary A relaxed and fun introduction into the college life.

Special Options The Princeton Review SAT preparation $380; SAT Verbal or Math $395; PSAT introduction $225; Course for study skills $195.

History Started twenty years ago, Exploration gives high school students a chance to spend summer vacation learning and having fun at the same time. They believe that summer learning should be a chance to explore areas not usually covered in school.

The Program Located on the beautiful campus of Wellesley college, Exploration offers high school students the opportunity to take courses that they would never find in a high school or college curriculum, courses like Silly

Love Songs, which investigates images of romance, or Lend Me Your Ear, which teaches you how to be a good peer counselor. The courses are fun and taught mainly by college students who can also tell you something about their own college experience.

The courses aren't super rigorous, but they serve as a great icebreaker for meeting your fellow students. In addition, you'll get to experience life on the campus of a prestigious private university. The program has a large number of extracurricular activities, from a series of mini-courses in creative arts to all kinds of sports. Through these activities and the trips throughout New England, you'll get the benefits of a travel program while learning in an on-campus environment.

If you want to work on your SAT scores, you can take The Princeton Review's course while going through the rest of the program. Exploration schedules The Princeton Review course during a free period, so you won't miss out on anything the on-campus experience has to offer.

 Allison Schwartz of New City, New York has attended the Exploration at Wellesley for two summers. She loved the experience and was especially pleased that she was able to meet people from all over the world: "Now if I travel anywhere in the country or anywhere in the world I have a place to stay." The program is set up so that it's easy to meet new people: "I hung out at this big hill with a tremendous tree with swings on it. We'd go there and listen to music. You only have three weeks there, even though it feels like you're there for a year. I was meeting people up to the last minute. You make friends and form relationships very quickly."

She also liked the fact that the teachers were very close to her own age: "The teachers were really great. Most were from the Northeast. They teach you not only about the subject, but also what it would be like to take that subject in college. What's really good is that the age difference between you and your teachers is only a few years. They don't act superior. They act like your friends."

While the program may not be for everyone, it's especially good for "people who are independent and are not afraid to experience new things. It's not a place for followers. You have to be able to think on your own and act independently. Conformity is looked down upon there. Everyone has to bring something of their own, whether its where you live or what you wear or how you act. You have to be different. It's what attracts people."

If you do go on the program, Schwartz advises that you "try things that you'd never do at home, because you don't live with these people. Be free."

Penn State

Address 900 Walt Whitman Road, Melville, NY 11747

Phone (800) 666-2556; (516) 424-1000

Fax (516) 424-0567

Cost $4,495 (Financial aid is available based on need.)

Ages 15–19; students completing grades 10, 11, and 12

Class Size Enrichment classes are 5–15. College-level classes are 15–60.

Size of program 500 students

Length of program 47 days

Application Deadline Early applications are preferred. Applications are processed in the order in which they are received. Spots usually fill by April.

Description On-campus program at Penn State University.

Summary A relaxed and unintimidating introduction to life at a Big Ten college.

Special Options The Princeton Review SAT preparation $395; Driver education $350; College counseling $245; Tennis $275-$495; Golf $450.

History Summer study at Penn State creates a relaxed atmosphere where students can ease into the life of a college freshman. The program combines Penn State college credit courses with special classes geared to high school students. By enrolling in this program you become part of the Big Ten college spirit.

The Program Students take college-level classes with Penn State students, and you can earn college credit. The courses run the gamut of college subjects with a few specialized courses to engage your interests. You might find a course about King Arthur and his court or on the theory of nutrition. Because the program allows you to take regular Penn State classes, you have a good deal of choice (approximately sixty college-credit courses).

The non-Penn State curriculum includes The Princeton Review's SAT course, creative writing, theater, engineering, rock 'n roll, and many other courses that might interest you. In addition, there's a special program "Pathways to College," which is taught by guidance counselors and helps you choose the best college. As part of this program, you'll spend three weekends visiting area campuses in upstate New York, Pennsylvania, and Washington, D.C.

Although you'll be taking courses, the academics are a bit challenging, but you'll have plenty of time to socialize and learn what it's like to live on your own. You'll make friends, play sports, enjoy nightly activities and weekend excursions, and hang out. Many students feel closer to the people they met at Penn State than to their high school friends.

 Jan Goodstein spent a summer at Penn State and found it to be a great time: "I liked it a lot. They bring you together with an icebreaker. Once you start making friends, it's a good time. When you get done with your classes, the whole afternoon is free, so you can hang out." The course work isn't too strenuous, so there's plenty of time left over after classes: "The biggest day of the week is three hours and fifteen minutes of work. The other days are two hours out of twenty-four. I can deal with that."

But a summer at Penn State isn't entirely about the classes; it's about meeting people and getting to know a college environment too: "You have to take one college course. I'm taking Health 60. It's a three-credit course. Some of the classes they offer are really hard. I never thought I'd be typing reports over the summer, but the work isn't a big deal. It doesn't stress me out."

Goodstein was really impressed with the range of activities: "They set up sports tournaments that the kids really get into. They choose up sides, and it's pretty serious. There's always something to do. Some nights we can go to clubs. You go in for free, and all the drinks are free, but there's no alcohol. They're strict with the curfew and drugs and alcohol. They kicked a few people out who had alcohol."

Penn State is an excellent choice if you're looking for a college experience without super-difficult academics. It's a window to the life at a Big Ten college.

Summer Discovery Programs

Address 1326 Old Northern Boulevard, Roslyn, NY 11576

Phone (800) 645-6611; (516) 621-3939

Fax (516) 625-3438

E-mail sdiscovery@aol.com

Cost $2,399–$4,299

Ages 15–19

Class Size 15–25 students

Size of program 120–300 students

Length of program 21–42 days

Application Deadline Early applications are preferred. Applications are processed in the order in which they are received.

Description On-campus programs at UCLA, University of Michigan, Georgetown, and the University of Vermont.

Summary A good, relaxing, pre-college experience. A great way to see what it's like to live on campus.

Special Options The Princeton Review SAT preparation $395; Various excursions $25-325; Tennis or golf lessons $125-200; Sailing $125.

History For over thirty years, the Musiker family has designed summer programs for high school students. They believe that a pre-college experience should engage more than just the mind. It should be a well-rounded experience including sports and recreation.

The Program Summer Discovery offers a range of summer programs that differ based primarily on location. If you attend the UCLA program, for example, you'll get to take courses for credit with other UCLA students. But all the courses at the other campuses are taught by Summer Discovery staff. In addition, the extracurricular activities are dependent on location. To give you an idea of how one of these programs works, we're going to describe the program at University of Michigan.

Located in Ann Arbor, perhaps the greatest college town in the nation, the University of Michigan is big enough to offer its students a diversity of courses and lifestyles. The Summer Discovery program takes advantage of the University of Michigan campus by giving you the opportunity to see outdoor movies in the park, or to hang out at the student union.

Each day, you will take two "enrichment" classes. These range from Princeton Review SAT courses to classes in all the traditional school subjects. You can study creative writing, social studies, mathematics, and even sociology or psychology. Because of its location at the University of Michigan, Discovery can offer special programs in architecture and visual arts that are connected to the university's schools in these areas.

Although the courses will challenge you to learn, they (with the exception of The Princeton Review) will offer very little outside homework. This will leave you plenty of time to partake in the different athletic and social events planned for you. You can study basketball under college basketball coaches, or study tennis with U of M's tennis coach. The weekends are set aside for trips to Chicago, Toronto, and camping. You'll get to explore the Midwest while experiencing the college life. Summer Discovery offers a nice, relaxing way to meet new people and to live on a college campus.

 Matthew Dellon, of New City, New York studied with Summer Discovery at UCLA. He was really impressed: "I thought it was great. If you don't have a good time, it's your own fault. You choose which classes to take. If you don't like something, don't take it. There's so much to do here. The activities in LA are amazing. You're in the entertainment capital of the world. Besides the planned activities like seeing The Tonight Show, there are residential counselors here who will take you on trips if you want to. Last Thursday, I went in a small van with a few friends to San Diego to watch the Padres play. It was great, especially since I love baseball."

He also really liked the classes: "My classes were great. I really enjoyed them. Besides the fact that getting up at 7:00 A.M. for a political science class is difficult, it was a very, very cool class if you like American politics. It was totally different from high school. I'm learning a lot more specific details, like that Washington died of syphilis rather than pneumonia. It's a different style of learning, a different atmosphere."

Summer Discovery has vans set up for impromptu trips. Dellon decided that he wanted to see the location of the most celebrated crime of the decade: "The second day I got here, I wanted to go on a trip to see OJ's house. It was one of the funniest things I've done in a long time. It was methodical, slow, and interesting. You want to look at it and think, he killed her there. Hmm. With a world event like this so close to the college, of course you're going to go."

ON-CAMPUS PROGRAMS IN ENGLAND

These programs are for those of you who want to study in England. They are usually designed so that you can take advantage of seeing England while studying at either Oxford or Cambridge. For example, you might study British law and then go to Parliament. These programs will also usually include a chance for an organized tour, but the main purpose of going is to learn in a different environment.

Academic Studies Associates (Oxford)

Address 355 Main Street, P.O. Box 800, Armonk, NY 10504-0800

Phone (800) 752-2250; (914) 273-2250

Fax (914) 273-5430

Cost $4,095 (Optional Paris five-day extension: $595, plus inter-European airfare. Transportation to and from London not included. ASA will arrange for low, group-rate travel.)

Ages 15–19

Class Size Most have fewer than 12 students

Size of program 160 students

Length of program 28 days

Application Deadline Early applications are preferred. Applications are processed in the order in which they are received.

Description Pre-college program at Oxford University in England.

Summary A great introduction to life at college and a chance to live abroad. With small, well-taught classes.

Special Options The Princeton Review's SAT preparation $350; Paris extension $595 plus airfare.

History Since 1983, ASA has been running pre-college enrichment programs in Oxford for high school students. They believe that a pre-college program should be a good place to learn new things and to learn what it's like to be a college students. A trip to Oxford with ASA will give you a great learning experience and a chance to explore some of Europe.

The Program The program at ASA is designed along the same lines as their domestic pre-college programs; the difference, and it's not a small one, is that it's in England. Not only will you get to experience another culture, but you'll be able to study subjects related to England with complimentary field trips to increase your understanding. For example, one of the classes teaches British art history. In this class you'll learn about the history of British art through visits to British museums. Studying the actual work of art is a great experience.

You can enjoy the beautiful environment of a museum, and truly understand what makes a masterpiece, well, a masterpiece. Or, you might study "Introduction to Law and Society," which features field trips to explore different aspects of the British legal system.

Another great feature of the Oxford program is the internship program. You can work within the fields of journalism, local government, and art. By actually working in Britain, you'll get a better sense of what the culture is like and how it differs from that of America.

Although you will be in England, you'll be associating mostly with American students. This can be a good way to comfortably begin your travels abroad by not being totally immersed in another culture. In addition, since you'll be studying British culture in a university system, you can get an educated and complete understanding of England.

The one-week extension in Paris is a visit to one of the most beautiful cities in the world. You'll stay in a three-star hotel and get a chance to visit the Eiffel Tower, Montmartre, and all the other Parisian sites.

 Elizabeth Naiman of Rye, New York, went on the ASA program to Oxford the summer before her senior year. She loved it: "It was the greatest month of my life. It gave me a chance to explore a new country and study at the greatest university in the world."

She especially liked her classes: "The teachers were great. One was a real Oxford professor, the other was an Oxford grad student who had studied at Yale. They were very knowledgeable. I took psychology and speech and debate. Psychology was really, really interesting. For that class we went out in the town of Oxford and they asked us to survey people. The professor was copying a survey done by a psychology professor in Yale in 1960. We asked people for their ideas about intelligence—what intelligence was. We stopped random British people in the street and asked what they thought everyday intelligence was. We got results and compared them with the study done by the Yale professor.

"The British people gave different answers than the Americans. The American people tended to focus a lot more on academic intelligence. The British people tended to think that everyday intelligence was measured by how well you dealt with people."

She got to speak with a member of Parliament: "We went to London where I spoke to a member of Parliament. He was a conservative and very straightforward. It was really interesting to hear about his job and the government."

While a trip to Oxford can be interesting to anyone, Naiman feels that it's better for those who "will appreciate being able to study in a great university. They gave us a lot of freedom so you have to be able to take that freedom and make the best of it. There's so much to see over there. I don't know why people who just want to sit in their dorm rooms would go."

If you do go, Naiman advises that you "go there with an open mind. Go there ready to learn a lot."

Summer Discovery (Cambridge)

Address 1326 Old Northern Boulevard, Roslyn, NY 11576

Phone (800) 645-6611; (516) 621-3939

Fax (516) 625-3438

E-mail sdiscovery@aol.com

Cost $4,199 (Transportation to and from London not included.)

Ages 15–19

Class Size 6–18 students

Length of program 21–42 days

Application Deadline Early applications are preferred. Applications are processed in the order in which they are received.

Description On-campus program at Cambridge, England.

Summary A relaxing pre-college experience in Europe. A great way to learn something about European culture and to experience college life in a foreign country.

Special Options The Princeton Review SAT preparation $395; Paris extension $995.

History From the designers of the Summer Discovery Program described on pages 149-150. This program in England offers credit courses with British instructors.

The Program The program in Cambridge takes advantage of its location on the beautiful campus. It offers two different curricula, one with a for-credit Cambridge class plus an optional enrichment class, the other with The Princeton Review SAT course plus an optional enrichment course. For those of you who are really gung-ho, you can take both The Princeton Review course and a for-credit course.

The for-credit courses are taught by Cambridge faculty, but remember the credit might not be accepted by your future college of choice. The courses available mirror the traditional collegiate liberal arts education, with offerings in the humanities and the social sciences. (No science courses are offered.) The enrichment courses are more creative and designed to be fun.

When you're not studying, you can explore Cambridge by taking walking tours. While you're there, you can attend the Cambridge international arts festival or the local film festival. Without much effort, you can explore this wonderful city and see the magnificent ways it differs from large American cities.

Even the athletic choices take advantage of the location. For an extra fee of $100, you can learn how to row on The Cam. This is a great way to get in shape and see Cambridge from the water. The Summer Discovery program at Cambridge offers you a mix of academics and social experiences that should make you a better prepared student when you enter college.

 Jeremy Cramer of Harrisburg, Pennsylvania, went with Summer Discovery to Cambridge. He loved the experience: "I had a great summer. It was a wonderful experience being overseas for a month, meeting kids from all over the world, taking courses for college credit. It was really an experience that not many kids my age are exposed to. It was really a treat having this experience.

"Classes were more challenging than the ones in high school because they were lecture-oriented. There was less student-teacher interaction. But the class was very interesting. Psychology has been one subject that I've been interested in since I was really young. The course was taught by a man in his late forties or fifties who plays the blues and is working on setting up a record contract with a big company in England. He was down-to-earth, interesting, and a very good teacher. In my paper, I psychoanalyzed Jeffrey Dahmer."

It was actually Cramer's second on-campus program with Summer Discovery. On his first, he met his girlfriend, and they both traveled to England together: "We met on a summer discovery in Michigan. We've stayed together all year. It's really enhanced our relationship. I'm away at boarding school. We had a lot of time to spend together."

One of his most memorable experiences was seeing the American Cemetery: "American Cemetery is home to 5,000 American soldiers who were stationed in England and died in World War II. It was pretty heart-wrenching. It had a huge stone memorial, a stone wall like the Vietnam Memorial. You really feel like you know all of them. It's a very solemn and special place. You just want to leave thanking all of them. They have gorgeous flowers all around. It's like a perfect serene setting, where all these people would want to be after they died in battle."

If you go on this trip, Cramer advises that you "meet as many people and take advantage of the wonderful opportunities that are available. Sit down and chat with as many of the Resident Counselors and tutors and people in the town as you can."

LEADERSHIP PROGRAMS

When you're in a tight situation with a group of friends, are you always the one who takes control of the situation? Do you have a knack for putting together a plan and executing it without a hitch? Well then, maybe you should consider attending a leadership camp. We list two programs that do excellent jobs at preparing you for potential leadership roles in society. You will learn the skills necessary to analyze difficult situations and think of creative solutions by looking at all angles of a problem.

Although the programs use law and government as a basis for their instruction, they are not designed only for people who want to be lawyers or politicians. No matter what you plan to do, where you plan to live, or who you want to work for, the skills that these programs teach you will be useful.

Both of these programs are academically oriented. If you're not into school, don't apply. They require a lot of academic work and a fair amount of responsibility to do that work. If, for example, you don't like to read, you may find these programs overwhelming.

The Junior Statesmen Summer Schools

Address 60 E. 3rd Ave., Suite 320, San Mateo, CA 94401

Phone (800) 334-5353; (415) 347-1600

Fax (415) 347-7200

Cost $2,200 (Financial aid is available. Over half of the students receive scholarships from $50 to $1,800. The awards are based on a combination of merit and need.)

Ages 14–18

Class Size Between 20 and 30 per class

Size of program Varies depending on program and location.

Length of program 28 days

Application Deadline Early applications are preferred. Applications are processed in the order in which they are received. A three-page essay, a high school transcript, and one teacher recommendation must accompany the application. The program is fairly selective, similar to a prestigious college.

Description A leadership and speaking program that teaches about the American political system and economics. Schools are located at the University of Texas/Austin, Stanford, Yale, and Georgetown Universities.

Summary A great program for those who are good students and who want to achieve. With challenging academics and a good deal of homework.

History For over fifty years, the Junior Statesmen summer schools have been preparing high school students to participate in our democratic society. The program aims to teach leadership skills, argument skills, and research skills.

The Program The programs at each university are fairly similar. You take courses six days a week. Each morning is spent studying American government for three hours. Each afternoon is spent studying public speaking. The evenings are spent participating in student debates. In addition, all the programs have field trips to hear speakers in action. The Georgetown program, however, is slightly different. Because of its location in Washington, D.C., the program focuses on listening to speakers in the area. You'll hear speeches by government officials and then critique their delivery.

The courses are taught by college professors who expect you to handle a tough workload. You'll be reading hundreds of pages, listening to speeches, going to classes, participating in debates, and at the same time doing research for a term paper. So as you might imagine, there isn't much time for socializing. On the other hand, the participants often bond together under the workload, and many alumni report remaining friends with people from the program for years afterward.

 Most students attending the program found the academics daunting at first. Allison Hughes of San Francisco, California remembers arriving on Sunday and being told to read the Constitution, the Declaration of Independence, and the first three chapters of the textbook all by Monday morning, when they would have a pop quiz. Within two or three days, she was upset, wondering if she would be able to keep up. But she ended up doing well, and returned to the program the next year. "A lot of people feel overwhelmed in the first week, but most people keep up. The only people who don't make it are those who don't want to be here."

Even though the academics are tough, the professors are great: "My teachers were fantastic. They were inspired and funny. And we got to hear some great speakers: (Noted economist) Milton Freedman, and (Former Reagan cabinet member) Ed Meese." After hearing the speakers, the students critique them with "whatever Aristotelian rhetoric that we were listening to." In other words, a program like this is not for the faint of heart. But future program participants should "not be intimidated. The program looks intimidating, but the professors are great. Hang out with them. Play basketball with them. You'll get a lot out of the program."

National Law and Leadership

Address 4800 North Federal Highway, Suite 106-D, Boca Raton, FL 33431

Phone (800) 394-6453

Cost $1,595 residential; $995 commuters; $95 course material fee

Ages 15–19

Class Size About 50 students

Size of program About 100 students

Length of program 12 days

Application Deadline Early applications are preferred. Applications are processed in the order in which they are received.

Description An academic program that teaches leadership skills through instruction in law and government. Programs are in Stanford and at American University in Washington, D.C.

Summary A great program to stretch your mind if you're academically motivated. Not just for those interested in law.

History Since 1989, National Law and Leadership has been educating students in how to think analytically. Through a course that teaches law and government, they will teach you effective problem-solving techniques that will help you later on. The program is intimate with excellent instruction.

The Program In 1996, National Law in Leadership is running a course that simulates the nomination of a justice of the Supreme

Court. If you follow the news, you can see how complicated this is in real life. A justice of the Supreme Court is supposed to be objective, and must follow the precedents from the last 200 years. But the law, like anything else, is full of gray areas, and presidents attempt to nominate justices whom they believe see gray in the "right" way. Members of Congress often disagree with one another, and a nomination fight ensues.

The 1996 program will feature one week in which some people are designated nominees, some advisors to the nominees, some senators, and some advisors to the senators. The nominees will each write a law brief telling their position on an issue that is vital to constitutional law (say, the first amendment).

Then the senators will question the nominees and try to keep a person of the "wrong" political persuasion from being named to the court.

The second week students prepare a case to be heard by the National Law and Leadership Supreme Court. The participants will try to win their case following all the procedures that would be necessary in the real Supreme Court. If this all seems dry and too academic for you, then this might not be the place to spend your time and money. However, if you want to learn some of the ways in which our government works, and if you want to learn the proper way to prepare and win an argument, then give this program a try.

Former participants in the program were impressed by how much it changed their way of thinking. The program attempts to teach students, to think analytically by using the Socratic method. This involves intense questioning to delve into the heart of an issue. The first night of the program is spent watching The Paper Chase, which shows some of how the Socratic method worked for one law professor at Harvard. "The actual program isn't as harsh," according to former participant John Orsini of Miami, Florida, "but it will challenge you. The professors will throw out questions and you have to figure out the answers on your own. It came down to me and my friends arguing about a case at night until we were blue in the face. But when we returned to class we found that we had been discussing the correct issues and were learning how to analyze a problem. No matter what your answer was, it wasn't enough. They would turn your questions back to you. It got to the point where I didn't want to ask another question. But eventually, everyone got the hang of it, and the whole process was incredibly rewarding."

The skills learned in the program had lasting value. Many of the participants feel that they are still using the skills in high school and college. "It taught me to go beyond the facts," said Orsini, "I learned to analyze and figure out the reasons behind events." He used the program as the subject for his college essay, and he got into Harvard.

National Law and Leadership is an excellent program to expand your mind and teach you how to think analytically about difficult subjects. If you're into academic challenges, give it a shot. Orsini advises to not be intimidated. "There's a lot of work here, but it's doable. And give the program everything you can. It'll be worth it."

SCIENTIFIC RESEARCH PROGRAMS

One of the best academic programs allows you to participate in scientific research. Imagine being part of an expedition to discover the secrets of Oregon's caves or the evolutionary history of China's elephants. The program that sets all this up is called Earthwatch, and it's an innovative example of a "win-win" situation. A scientist will propose an expedition, and a group of people will pay for the privilege of helping collect necessary data. For less than many of the other programs in the book, you could be part of an expedition that discovers something cool, and all your money will go to fund it.

IT'S EVEN LESS EXPENSIVE THAN IT SEEMS

In addition, because your money goes to a nonprofit, scientific expedition, your entire fee is tax-deductible. This means that depending on your family's tax bracket, you can get back as much as 39 percent of the cost of your trip from the federal government. Neat, huh? Besides the fact that you'll be helping scientists engage in important research, you'll be funding the expedition as well. And you'll learn a great deal.

BUT IT'S NOT FOR EVERYBODY

Earthwatch is not a program exclusively for high school students. It's for people sixteen and older, so you will be around many people who are much older. This means that unless you're mature enough to spend a few weeks hanging out with adults, these projects may not be for you. In addition, you'll be working in the field and sleeping in some not-so-posh places. Don't expect any luxuries. These trips are set up with a purpose, and you will work hard and for long hours.

Earthwatch

Address 680 Mount Auburn Street, P.O. Box 403, Watertown, MA 02272-9924

Phone (800) 776-0188; (617) 926-8200

Fax (617) 926-8532

E-mail info@earthwatch.org

Cost $595–$2,395 (Need-based aid available to students. Participants are responsible for travel to the staging area.)

Ages 16–80

Size of group Depends on the project

Length of program 7–21 days

Application Deadline You must first become a member of Earthwatch. You then choose specific programs in which you would like to participate.

Description Research trips all over the world in agriculture, archaeology, art and architecture, botany, cultural anthropology, ecology, entomology, ethnomusicology, geology, health and nutrition, herpetology, ichthyology, mammalogy, marine ecology, marine mammalogy, ornithology, paleontology, resource management, sociology, volcanology, and wildlife management.

Summary A chance to help out scientists with their research. Not just for high school students. No need for any scientific knowledge or skills.

History A nonprofit organization started in 1972, Earthwatch is one of the largest private sponsors of scientific research in the world. It organizes expeditions that are staffed and paid for by volunteers. Although the primary goal of an Earthwatch expedition is to engage in scientific research, it also gives the participants an unforgettable experience.

The Program It's difficult to describe a typical project since Earthwatch projects happen all over the world in every conceivable scientific field, but we're going to describe their research program in dolphin intelligence in Honolulu, Hawaii. It's certainly one of the more luxurious expeditions: you'll be staying in a two bedroom apartment with a view of the harbor. You'll work five days a week, but you'll have weekends free to explore Honolulu. Although your research tasks will be organized, you'll be totally on your own in your free time. Since Earthwatch is primarily a research project, nobody will be concerned about your leisure activities.

This particular research project has been going on for years and its goal is to measure dolphin intelligence. You've probably heard tales of the remarkable intelligence of dolphins. If you volunteer to work on this project you'll see for yourself. Dolphins can remember, communicate, and sometimes even understand. By helping with the arduous task of recording the dolphins' behavior during different tests, you'll provide valuable assistance to a scientific researcher. Sure, a lot of the job will consist of organizing equipment and entering data, but you'll also get opportunities to work directly with the dolphins.

As a learning experience, Earthworks cannot be beat, but it's not for everyone. You will not be supervised when you're not working, and because you won't be around other people your age, you must be able to figure out what to do with your own time.

In the summer after his sophomore year, Nathaniel Rayl of Vermont went to North Carolina as part of an Earthwatch study of the black bears of the region. Through some luck and a well-written essay, he received a full scholarship to the program. An anonymous donor at his school offered a scholarship to both a student and a teacher. According to Rayl, "They were studying the black bears and trying to figure out what determines a bear's territory and why some of their territories are larger than others. There were eighteen of us, four or five my age. Everyday we were assigned a trail. And we'd walk these trails to see what bears were caught in the snare. When you catch one they'd tranquilize it, weigh it, and attach a collar with an antenna on it."

Although the expedition didn't run across too many bears, Rayl did find one that left him with an unforgettable experience: "This friend of mine and I caught this 300-pound bear. There were these trails, but the traps were off the trails to protect the hikers from the bears and the bears from the hikers. We were walking toward this trap, and all of sudden there was this black blur that was running around, charging at us. We were supposed to leave right away, but we stayed and took pictures. I had this really loud camera, and it just aggravated the bear. It was kind of nerve-racking, because we thought it might get away. Later on, when they tried to tranquilize the bear it wouldn't go down. They had to give it enough tranquilizers for a 1,000-pound bear. Even though the researchers were a little mad, everything worked out. Nobody got killed." Of course, the bear would have been a lot happier had Rayl not come along.

Rayl was impressed with the diversity of the participants. They were from all over the world. He feels that an Earthwatch expedition is good for anyone, even if he or she isn't into science. His one piece of advice for anyone going on one of these trips, however, is to "bring something to do. I didn't bring a Walkman or anything like that, and it got claustrophobic staying in that tent with the same five people all the time. I brought some heavy school reading material, but after a day of work, who wants to read anything difficult?"

7 Travel

TAKING OFF

Okay, so you've decided that it's time to leave your one-horse town and head off to lands unknown. What are the options?

ON YOUR OWN?

We'd like to recommend that you think very carefully before taking this option. While the notion of backpacking around the country is certainly romantic, it's also extremely dangerous if you're not in an organized program or at least traveling with other experienced hikers. The dangers that might await you miles and miles from home are not to be faced alone or taken lightly. Besides, a good guide can give you insight into an area that you can't get on your own.

If you do decide to head off without an established program, take measures to protect yourself. Always tell somebody where you are going, how you will get there, and when you expect to arrive. If something happens when you are traveling, you cannot expect help unless someone knows your itinerary.

Do Not Go Totally by Yourself

It's just too dangerous, not to mention lonely.

Don't Hitchhike

Although thirty to forty years ago a lot of students explored the country by hitchhiking, it's far too dangerous today.

Bring Enough Money (and a Credit Card if Possible)

If you plan on traveling in the United States, bring a bank machine card. It will be usable almost anywhere. If you don't have one, bring traveler's checks.

Know Where You'll Be Sleeping

Although it might seem easy and romantic to sleep on the road somewhere, it's not safe. Plan well, and make reservations whenever possible. Find out if there are youth hostels located in the vicinities of your destinations and mark them on a map. There are 260 youth hostels in the U.S. and Canada, and not only are they safe, reasonably clean places to stay, they're also cheap. The International Youth Hostel Federation (IYHF) has hostels nationwide and internationally. Call them at (202) 783-6161 for more information about where their hostels are located, or 1-(800) 444-6111 to make reservations (highly recommended).

Plan Short Trips

Until you get the hang of travel, it's a good idea to go on shorter trips. If things aren't working out, you know you'll be home soon, and you'll get through any problems you might have. It also might be likely that your parents will let you venture off with a group of your friends on a shorter trip first.

Get a Good Guidebook

If you decide to go on your own, you should get some good advice. Especially if you'll be in another country. We think Rick Steves' *Europe Through the Back Door* is a great book to check out. It tells you the best way to find unusual places and how to learn about the culture while you travel. His advice can be extremely helpful when you are planning a trip. Steves is also the author of a book called *Europe 101*, which shows you how the sites you see are related to European History.

You also might want to pick up *Lonely Planet* guide books, which give hints on how to find out-of-the-way places while backpacking. Also worth checking out is the *Let's Go* series. Written by college students traveling through Europe and the U.S., these guides will tell you the best places to see, stay, and eat, and since they're written by people close to your age, you can be pretty secure that the advice will be useful to you.

Another good idea is to read up on the differences in culture between America and your planned destination. *The Survival Kit for Overseas Living: For Americans Planning to Live and Work Abroad* by L. Robert Kohls is an excellent guide to what you might run into overseas. It will instruct you in fairly complete detail on how America differs from other countries, and how you can either avoid or deal with culture shock.

The Exchange Student Survival Kit by Bettina Hansel is a great guide for students who want to spend time abroad. Hansel, who worked for American Field Service (AFS) for a number of years, relates the experiences of students in many different cultures.

You can't buy all of these books in a regular bookstore, but you can purchase them directly from their publisher:

> *Intercultural Press*
> *16 U.S. Route One, P.O. Box 700, Yarmouth, ME 04096*
> *Phone: (207) 846-5168*
> *Fax: (207) 846-5181*

Get a Student Identification Card

If you do travel abroad, you need to get an International Student Identity Card from the Council on International Educational Exchange (CIEE). These cards cost $16 and entitle you to student discounts in over ninety countries (including on

plane tickets), some basic insurance, access to a toll-free number if you get in trouble, and they're good until you turn 26.

CIEE's Information and Student Services Department
205 East 42nd Street, New York, NY 10017
(212) 661-1450

The following is a list of phone numbers where you can find the CIEE. They can be extremely helpful in finding discount fares and suggesting the best way to set up a trip.

Arizona		**Michigan**	
Tempe	(602) 966-3544	Ann Arbor	(313) 998-0200
California		**Minnesota**	
Berkeley	(510) 848-8604	Minneapolis	(612) 379-2323
Long Beach	(310) 598-3338	**New York**	
Los Angeles	(310) 208-3551	New York	(212) 661-1450
Palo Alto	(415) 325-3888		
San Diego	(619) 270-6401	**North Carolina**	
San Francisco	(415) 421-3473	Durham	(919) 286-4664
Sherman Oaks	(818) 905-5777	**Ohio**	
Colorado		Columbus	(614) 294-8696
Boulder	(303) 477-8101	**Oregon**	
Connecticut		Portland	(503) 228-1900
New Haven	(203) 562-5335	**Pennsylvania**	
Washington, D.C.	(202) 337-6464	Philadelphia	(610) 282-0343
Florida		**Rhode Island**	
Miami	(305) 670-9261	Providence	(401) 331-5810
Georgia		**Texas**	
Atlanta	(404) 377-9997	Austin	(512) 472-4931
		Dallas	(214) 363-9941
Illinois		**Washington**	
Chicago	(312) 951-0585	Seattle	(206) 632-2448
Evanston	(708) 475-5070		
Louisiana		**Wisconsin**	
New Orleans	(504) 866-1767	Milwaukee	(414) 332-4740
Massachusetts			
Amherst	(413) 256-1261		
Boston	(617) 266-1926		
Cambridge	(617) 497-1497		

GET WITH THE PROGRAM

Luckily, no matter what your interests, there's a travel program for you. There are travel programs that take you to the most beautiful American scenery imaginable. There are biking programs that allow you to see the same scenery and test your endurance, as well. There are even wilderness programs in which you get closer to that scenery than you may ever have imagined wanting to.

And once you decide how you will travel, you must decide where you want to go. Programs are offered throughout the United States and in nearly every other country in the world. You can go to the Turquoise Trail or Timbuktu, to Niagara Falls or the Nile.

What About the Cost?

Unfortunately, these programs aren't cheap, but the prices are competitive with any organized program. If you were considering camp, but realize that you would rather travel, you won't have to pay that much more.

Make a Personal Choice

To help you decide what is right for you, we are going to discuss the ins and outs of each type of program. The decision will be yours. What kind of person are you? Do you like things to be organized or do you want to be in control? You have to decide what is best for you, and then pick a program that offers it.

CROSS-COUNTRY TRIPS IN THE UNITED STATES

One way to get around the country is on a tour sponsored by one of the companies mentioned in the following paragraphs. However, there are some issues you will want to consider beforehand. First, although well-guided and well-planned, these trips are expensive. Second, most of the traveling you'll do will probably be in an air-conditioned bus. If you still need Dramamine pills to endure a short ride in your parents' car, then this might not be your ideal trip. But if you don't mind riding and crave structure, such a trip might be perfect. Accommodations tend to be in hotels, or in large, roomy tents with comfortable cots. Great food is the norm, and there's always an enthusiastic counselor around to inform you about your destination. Bus trips are great if you want to see the country from ground level and take part in some really fun activities along the way, like white-water rafting, horseback riding, or water skiing. You're not under the ever-watchful eye of your parents, but you also don't have to take the risks involved with sticking out your thumb on Route 66. It's a happy medium.

How Long Is Long Enough?

The next question is how long you want to be gone. For most people, this decision will be made by cost. But even if that's not a consideration, you still might want to consider a shorter program your first time around. If you've never traveled before, a month or more can be a long time to be away from home. Even though the trips that we list will provide you with many of the comforts of home, you might find yourself a bit homesick on a six-week trek around the country. Save the epic odyssey for your second trip.

American Trails West

Address 92 Middle Neck Road, Great Neck, NY 11021

Phone (800) 645-6260; (516) 487-2800

Fax (516) 487-2855

E-mail atwtours@aol.com

Cost $2,995–$5,295 (Airfare to and from starting point not included. Some trips include flights between segments. In such cases, airfare within trip is included.)

Ages 13–17 (Participants for all trips are grouped by age.)

Size of group 40

Length of program 21–42 days

Application deadline Early applications are preferred. Applications are processed in the order in which they are received.

Description Motorcoach trips to different areas of the country, including Alaska and Hawaii.

Summary A great way to see the country in style and to see as many sites as possible.

History Started in 1965, American Trails West is the largest and perhaps the best of the companies offering cross-country bus trips. Because of its size, it can offer services and trips that its competitors can't match. And because so many students travel on their trips, they are able to ensure that you hang out with people your own age from all over the country. With thousands of happy campers served, it's no wonder that ATW keeps attracting high school students eager to explore. American Trails West is about variety. They have trips to all areas of the U.S. where you stay in camp-grounds, on campus, or sometimes in hotels.

The Program To give you an idea of what an ATW trip is like, we're going to describe their thirty-day "Discoverer" trip. You'll start by taking a jet plane to Denver and then spending nine days in "Big Sky" country. There you'll meet the other participants and travel to the Black Hills of South Dakota where you'll see Mount Rushmore. You'll see a rodeo, Yellowstone National Park, Grand Canyon of Yellowstone, Jackson Hole, Grand Teton National Park, and Salt Lake City. While you're in the area, you'll go on an alpine slide, hike through the mountains, see a sound and light show, and more. During your trip you'll stay in tents with either a cot or a mattress or both.

After Big Sky country, you take a jet to Northern California where you'll see San Francisco and all of its great sights, from Chinatown to Alcatraz. In San Francisco, you can see the Hard Rock Cafe, go to a disco, or just explore the streets. Then it's off to a resort lakeside campground where you'll get to lie on the beach, water ski, and rest up for a visit to Yosemite National Park.

After this, you'll be LA-bound, where you'll stay on the UCLA campus, watch a baseball game, see a Hollywood taping, and go to Disneyland. Then, San Diego, where you'll see the famed San Diego zoo and other great attractions. Next you go to Nevada and the Zion, Bryce, and Grand Canyons. Hiking, mountain biking, and rafting on the Colorado River are some of the adventures you'll be able to have on the way to Denver and your flight home.

 Josh Zinns of Boca Raton, Florida went with American Trails West on their California Sunset trip and loved it: "It was an amazing trip. It was a good blend. It was half hotel and half camping trip. So you got to be outdoors and also spend some time in cities. I can honestly say it was the best summer of my life. I really had a great time. Next year I'm going with ATW to Alaska."

Zinns saw a bunch of amazing sites, but one stuck out in his mind: "The coolest thing I saw was the Grand Canyon. You have to see it. It was just amazing. It really made you feel small. It's this amazing formation in the middle of nowhere. It's a little scary standing on the edge of it, but we went to the top and took pictures."

He was also impressed with how well-run the trip was. There were things to do at any time of the day, and even the food was exceptional: "It's prepared fresh every day. The meals are really varied. We had Mexican food, Italian food, chicken teriyaki, pasta—all you can eat, all fresh."

Zinns feels that an American Trails West trip is for everybody: "Everybody should go. There's something for everyone on the trip. We had athletes, intellectuals, and everyone had a good time." His advice for a future ATW traveler is to "do everything that you can. If you have a choice whether to do an activity or not, don't sit it out, because you'll miss out on a lot. Also, appreciate what's going on whether it's rainy or sunny. Have a great time."

North American Trails

Address 302 Rutland Street, Carlisle, MA 01741

Phone (800) 356-3591; (508) 371-2566

Cost $1,750–$4,450

Ages 13–16

Size of group 20–40 depending on the trip

Length of program 17–42 days

Application deadline Early applications are preferred. Applications are processed in the order in which they are received.

Description Bus trips around the United States.

Summary A fun and easy way to see the country. Excellent for your first trip.

History Started by Bob Accetta in 1981, North American Trails puts together cross-country trips for seventh to eleventh graders. The trips are incredibly well-supervised with one of the two directors of the program always on the bus. North American Trails believes that a cross-country trip should include elements of camping in it, and because of this you will get a safe but relatively authentic outdoors experience.

The Program A cross-country trip is about sightseeing, and North American Trails offers plenty of it. To give you a sense of the scope of one of these trips, we're going to describe what you'll see on the first half of the thirty-day *Northwestern Discovery*. You'll start by flying into Denver, Colorado, where you'll meet your group and board the bus to travel to the Black Hills region of South Dakota. There you'll see Mt. Rushmore and the Badlands National Park. After which, you'll go to the Rocky Mountains, where you'll tour Grand Tetons National Park, Yellowstone National Park, and (on horseback) Glacier National Park.

Then, it's off to the Canadian Rockies, where you'll see the Calgary Stampede, Jasper National Park, and spend some time in the city of Vancouver, British Columbia. Back in the U.S., you'll go to Seattle, Mt. Rainier National Park, and Mt. Saint Helens. Then it's white-water rafting in Oregon. If you get the feeling that you'll see a lot of America in a short time, you're right. And it's not as if you'll be doing nothing on the bus between trips. Activities are planned to keep the time passing fast.

The evenings of the trip are designed to give you a chance to kick your shoes off and relax. The days are not. On the *Northwestern Discovery* trip, you'll rollerskate, play miniature golf, bowl, go-cart, ice skate, go to amusement parks, see movies, go to ball games, eat in Chinatown in Vancouver, and just hang out around the campfire singing songs and telling stories.

 Jen Tarnoff, of Philadelphia, PA went on North American Trails' 21-day Atlantic Connection. She enjoyed it a great deal: "It was amazing. When I went, nobody else was from Philadelphia. Everybody was really warm and caring. They were open to meeting new people. It was a lot of fun."

Her favorite part was the white-water rafting: "I had never been, and we went on a level 4 out of 5. The only thing I'd ever seen was The River Wild. [A 1994 movie with Meryl Streep.] Basically, when I got there, everyone in the boat was teasing me because I had never been. The first wave was amazing. It was such a rush. I would do it every day if I could."

She also really liked the counselors: "The head was an angel. With the amount of stress that she had, she was so calm. Most of them were really nice and loved the outdoors. Everybody else was terrific. I kept up with one of the counselors; I'm going to see her this weekend."

While she thinks the trip was fantastic, she doesn't think it's for everyone. "I think that only outgoing people who love the outdoors and like trying new things should go. You've got to be willing to try things that you haven't tried before, like white-water rafting or horseback riding. You have to be open-minded to meet new people. You have to love to have fun."

If you're going on this trip, Tarnoff has the following advice: "Don't think that you're higher than anyone else. Be willing to include anyone in your group. Besides making your summer a lot of fun, you can make someone else's really fun too."

BIKE TRIPS

If you want a little less comfort and a lot more exercise, consider one of the programs that allows you to bike around the country. These programs put you with a group of ten or so other high school students, and together you start at a home base somewhere and pedal away. As you might imagine, the fun in these programs is getting there. And while you may see some amazing sights, you will be spending most of your time on your bike.

This, of course, is not necessarily a bad thing; it just should help put things in perspective. When you check out these programs, look for ones that aren't super ambitious, and that are located in areas where there are a lot of places to see in a small space. For example, while it might be beautiful to travel through Colorado, everything is so far apart that you won't get to see much of the state. On the other hand, New England is a relatively small area with many great sights next to each other. Make sure that the itinerary is reasonable.

Don't Lie to Yourself

Although these programs have special trips for inexperienced bikers and will give you a bike trip to match your ability, you will be on a bike most of the trip. This means that there will be some days when the wind is in your face and you don't get very far. On the other hand, you will have the satisfaction of traveling under your own power, and you will leave the trip in much better shape than when you arrived.

Just like the bus trips, there's a biking trip for just about everybody anywhere. There are mountain-bike trips that have you biking off-road through the woods as well as trips in Europe and almost anywhere in the world.

The Biking Expedition

Address P.O. Box 547, Henniker, NH 03242

Phone (800) BIKING X ; (603) 428-7500

Fax (603) 428-3414

Cost $1,494–$3,995

Ages 12–18 (Participants for the more popular trips are grouped by age.)

Size of group 8–13 students with 2–3 leaders per group

Length of program 14–64 days

Application deadline Early applications are preferred. Applications are processed in the order in which they are received. Early enrollments get a discount.

Description Road-biking and mountain-biking trips through different areas of the United States. Choices range from easy to very difficult in various locations.

Summary A chance to ride across some of the most beautiful scenery of the United States. For both beginners and experts.

History Since 1973, The Biking Expedition has sent thousands of young people on trips around the country. Offering both road bicycling and mountain biking, The Biking Expedition will give you a chance to test your limits, and you will return with legs of steel.

The Program Although TBE's programs range from beginner to "challenge," we're going to describe a moderate trip, a twenty-seven day road bike tour around Nova Scotia and Prince Edward Island. You'll start from Halifax and then cycle through the green farmland of the Shubernacadie River valley. Then you'll ride the tide upriver to the Bay of Fundy, where it's windsurfing and rejuvenation for the idyllic ride around Prince Edward Island. Here you'll get to go deep sea fishing and horseback riding.

Then it's on to the Northeast shore where you'll dismount for a two-day sea kayak trip on which there's ample opportunity for whale-spotting. The end of the trip is in Halifax, the capital of Nova Scotia and a pretty fun town with a rich maritime culture.

On a typical mountain bike programs like *Mountain Bike: North Colorado*, you'll get a thorough mountain-biking experience, even if you're a beginner. The trails range from easy to extremely difficult, culminating in an adventurous trip 13,000 feet above sea level beyond the tree line. In addition to the biking, you'll get to white-water raft on the Arkansas river, rock climb, and hike through Rocky Mountain National Park.

Alex Eule of Washington, D.C. went on the Biking Expeditions Pacific Coast bike trip from Seattle to San Francisco and was delighted with the experience: "I loved it. I had a great time. I loved biking. I got along really well with the people on the trip, and the leaders were great."

His most vivid memory is of when the group did a century, a hundred miles of biking: "We went from Eureka, California and went 100 miles and stopped, to the middle of nowhere. That was a great day of biking. There was a real sense of accomplishment because it was the last day."

Because the group was so small—nine cyclists and three leaders—they developed their own themes and inside jokes. "We had a theme, a Safeway theme. We must have stopped at twenty-five or thirty Safeways on the trip. There wasn't a town without a Safeway, and there wasn't a Safeway without a town."

Although this trip might not be for everyone, "someone who likes to be outdoors should go, someone who is adventuresome and ready to roll with the punches. Everything is not totally planned out. Also, if you're in pretty good shape, you'll probably enjoy yourself more. You can't mind sleeping in tents for a month. You have to be self-sufficient."

His advice for anyone going on the trip is to "be totally open at the beginning of the trip; be ready to accept the people on the trip. It's really important that everyone gets along with each other. Two people fighting would ruin the trip."

Interlocken—Crossroads Student Travel

Address Interlocken RR2 Box 165, Hillsboro, NH 03244

Phone (603) 478-3166

Fax (603) 478-5260

Cost $2,395–$3,680 (Transportation to and from starting point not included.)

Ages 12–18

Size of group 13 students with 2 leaders

Length of program 28–42 days

Application deadline Early applications are preferred. Applications are processed in the order in which they are received.

Description Road-biking trips to the Pacific Coast, Quebec, Italy, and France. Mountain biking in the Canadian Rockies.

Summary A chance for adventure and challenge. A great way to learn about the environment and meet people.

History Started in 1967 by Interlocken (an international summer camp), Crossroads Student travels gives you a chance to engage in cross-cultural exploration and physical challenges. The biking trips are difficult but manageable for the average high school student.

The Program Crossroads offers four different biking expeditions: three in North America, and one in Europe. We're going to give a brief description of their Pacific Coast trip from Portland to San Francisco. The 750-mile trip is completed in six weeks with a few stops in between, which means that the pace is fairly moderate. You'll start in Portland and travel through Oregon along the Pacific coast. There, you'll ride through many small West Coast towns and get to relax after each long, hot ride with a swim in the Pacific Ocean.

Then it's off to the Klamath River where you'll white-water raft through some serious class 4 white water. After this break from the road, you'll head for California where you'll get to attempt a century ride (100 miles in one day) amidst the immense trees of the Redwood Forest Preserve. Eventually, you'll ride over the Golden Gate Bridge into San Francisco, where you'll stay in a hostel and explore the city.

The itinerary for a crossroads trip is fairly relaxed, so, as you go, you and the rest of the group can make changes in the plans. You might see a town that you want to explore, or a beach that looks inviting. The point of a Crossroads trip is the journey, not the destination.

 Delia Langley of New Hampshire went with Interlocken on the Pacific Coast trip: "It was very exciting. We woke up and biked. We took side trips. We went to the sand dunes in Oregon. They're these big mountains of sand. They were at a campground that we went to, and we walked up them and then ran down them."

Although most of the time was spent biking, "we made our own schedule. If we were too tired we took a rest day. The most miles we did was seventy during the day." The day they did the seventy miles, they had planned to do 100 but "there were a lot of hills, which made it hard because we carried our luggage on our bikes. We took a lot of breaks."

The bike trips are best for athletic types. According to Langley, however, there were all types on her trip. "There were a lot of different people. There were mellow people and active people." Her advice to anyone going on an Interlocken bike trip is to "keep going. A couple of people backed out and left. Just keep going and trying. Eventually, you'll make it. It took a lot of energy and work to do it, but I made it, and I was really surprised that I did."

Odyssey

Address P.O. Box 5456, Hanover, NH 03755

Phone (800) 544-3216; (603) 643-3323

Fax (603) 643-4249

Cost $3,630–$5,730 (Round-trip airfare from NYC included. Bike rentals range from $160 to $225. Saddlebags and handlebar bags rent for $100.)

Ages 14–18

Size of group 15 participants per group with two staff members

Length of program 23–37 days

Application deadline Early applications are preferred. Applications are processed in the order in which they are received. Final deadline is April 30.

Description A biking exploration of Europe.

Summary A great way to improve your French or Spanish speaking and to explore Europe. Because you will be on bikes, you will have more interactive experiences with the people and get a complete sense of what the culture of the host country is like.

History Since 1985, Odyssey Adventures has been offering bike tours of Europe. Although the physical activity will be hard at times, it's not the focus of the trip. Most of the time, you'll be exploring European towns and villages and meeting people from these beautiful and culturally vital areas. Also, for an additional $875, you get one week of intensive language instruction to prepare you to meet the locals. (You must have studied one year of French to qualify.)

The Program The Cycling in France "C" trip is one part of Odyssey's "A" trip, a transcontinental trip around Europe. If you have already studied French, you can start with a language refresher in Tours to better prepare you for your trip. Otherwise, you'll start in the Loire Valley, where you'll learn about the cultural differences that you might encounter on your trip. Then you'll bike through the region. A van will follow and keep you supplied with food, so you won't have to worry about purchasing or carrying supplies. The roads chosen are quiet, and you'll ride through quaint French villages and pass gorgeous sunflower fields. You'll stay in campgrounds that are frequented by French villagers. One of the strengths of the Odyssey program is that they avoid tourist traps and place you in situations where you'll actually meet "the natives."

After the Loire Valley, you'll head for Burgundy, where you'll see vineyards in the heart of the best wine-making region in the world. Then it's off to Switzerland and Zermatt. You'll finish the biking part of the trip by ascending the Matterhorn, the most famous of the Swiss Alps. The last few days are spent in Paris, exploring and eating some great food. In Paris, even a simple omelet can be heavenly.

By the time you get done with the trip, not only will your legs be strong, but your language skills and cross-cultural communication will have improved. The Odyssey people believe that the best way to see a foreign country is by bike, and for some people, they are correct.

Bree Bradner went on the Odyssey Transcontinental Adventure through Europe and found the five-week tour a great way to see Europe and to travel. One nice feature of the Odyssey bike trips is that the groups change as you go. You pick destinations that you want to see, and as you go through different areas, you travel with new people. This can keep the group dynamics interesting.

In Europe the cars will actually move out of the way to avoid bikers. Even though most of the trip was on back roads, the little bit that was on main streets felt fairly safe. According to Bradner, "In Europe, even when the roads are busy, drivers have a completely different mentality than in America. Drivers would hit another car rather than a bicycle. They appreciate bicycles."

The actual biking was fairly easy. According to Bradner: "You didn't have to be in good shape. We rode an average of twenty-five to forty miles a day, which isn't that much. We rode at a pretty slow pace." But the biking wasn't the goal; seeing Europe was. One girl had never biked before. "She learned on the spot. She did pretty well, but she didn't like going downhill very much." The trip was "good for people who want to bike, but aren't really experienced at it. If you want to be casual and learn about European culture, Odyssey is a good way to go."

TRAVEL ABROAD

There are a large number of travel programs to choose from, but we've broken them down into three types: travel/tour programs, language programs, and community service programs. Before you decide which way to travel, you have to decide what you want to get out of the experience. The programs range from those that show you the sights to those that put you in direct contact with the people you're visiting. Here's a brief rundown of the different types of travel:

Travel/Tour

A travel/tour program is a great way to see a foreign country and meet some of the people who live there. The entire point of a program like this is to show you a country; you don't have to worry about learning the language or studying anything else (although we highly recommend it, even if you just do a little research on your own. It can only add to the depth of your encounters). The goal is to have an experience in travel.

Language Programs

These are intensive programs that give you a chance to improve your foreign language skills. The programs vary in intensity. Some make you speak a foreign language the whole time you're at the program. Some are more like taking college courses in France or Mexico. Even if you aren't very good at a language when you go, you'll improve rapidly. One summer of these programs is about equivalent to a year or more of high school instruction. There's no way you'll ever learn how to speak a language fluently unless you practice in a country where the language is spoken.

Community Service

These programs send you somewhere and give you a chance to do some kind of community service. They're great opportunities to travel and help people at the same time. Because you will work directly with the people you're helping, you'll get some of the benefits of an intensive travel program, and you'll get to meet people you would otherwise not get a chance to meet. These programs, because they are in poor areas, require a great deal of maturity. You'll have to understand the difficult living conditions that exist in third-world countries, and you'll have to live like that yourself.

Be Ready for Anything

No matter what type of program you pick, you'll be exposed to a different lifestyle from the one you're used to. Every participant we've talked with has offered the

same piece of advice. Be open-minded, willing to accept differences, and on the look-out for any chance to do something new and strange.

By getting out of the country, you will not only gain a better understanding of international affairs, you will have a better sense of our own culture and history. Besides, you will meet people who have grown up in environments totally different from your own.

Is it Right for You?

Not everyone will gain from an international experience. You might not have the temperament. Remember, you're going to be in an environment that is unfamiliar to you with people who may not speak English. Will you get frustrated when you're trying to understand someone talking in a language you don't understand? If you can even imagine yourself saying "Speak English, damn it!" foreign travel isn't for you. Being flexible is key to travel abroad. Here are some things to think about.

Can You Deal with a Different Diet?

Will you be able to, say, eat a bowl of hot rice soup for breakfast? If you go abroad, you'll have to be prepared for different foods. One student traveler we know saw the father of his host family take the live beating heart of a fish, drop it into some vodka, and quaff the whole thing down. (Luckily, the traveler wasn't offered the same delicacy.) You should be prepared to eat food that is different from what you're used to.

What About Sanitary Facilities?

Although many cultures use Western style toilets, some don't. Can you picture yourself using a toilet that is little more than a hole in the ground?

Can You Handle Stricter Rules of Etiquette?

Different cultures have different rules of etiquette. What might be acceptable in the United States might be considered a horrendous faux pas in another country. For example, in certain Asian cultures even the language has different forms to express different levels of politeness. You will have to be willing to be more careful about how you speak to different people.

Will You Be Able to Deal with Extreme Conditions?

Depending on where you go, you could be somewhere with people who are very poor. You'll need a great deal of maturity, intelligence, and flexibility to deal with certain situations that you might not be used to.

TRAVEL/TOUR PROGRAMS

These programs are for those of you who want to see a foreign country and learn more than just where the famous sights are. The programs range from those that put you up at fancy hotels to those that have you living in hostels and student homes. Before you choose a program, decide just what type of traveler you are. Do you want to live like the people you're visiting and explore their way of life or do you want to see as much of the country as you can? Then go through the listings and decide which ones interest you. Call up the organizations' phone numbers and ask for brochures. Get names of other participants and talk to them.

Being in a foreign country is a lot different from being in the U.S. People might not speak English (it's better to expect that they won't), and you will be forced to use every bit of your brain power to get around. The more the program leaves up to you, the harder, and more memorable, your experience will be.

AFS (American Field Service)

Address 220 East 42nd Street, 3rd floor, New York, NY 10017

Phone (800) AFS-INFO; (212) 949-4242

Cost $2,895–$3,795 (Round-trip airfare from NYC, Miami, or LA included. Provides significant scholarships to underserved minority groups.)

Ages 14–18

Size of group 5–60 (depending on the program)

Length of program 28–42 days

Application deadline March 15.

Description Travel and homestay programs in Argentina, Belgium-Flanders, Chile, Costa Rica, Ecuador, Finland, Germany, Italy, Latvia, Netherlands, Paraguay, Spain, Thailand, and Turkey.

Summary A challenging homestay program that requires a good deal of responsibility. You may face many of the challenges on your own.

History AFS is one of the oldest and largest travel programs in the country. It offers some of the longest homestays in the business, and expects a great deal of responsibility from its participants. You will, without a doubt, learn a great deal about the day-to-day life and culture of the place you're visiting.

The Program AFS programs can vary a great deal depending on which country you choose to travel to, but the basic premise is the same. You fly with other AFS participants to the city where orientation will be held. There you learn something about the area you'll be staying in, and get some quick language instruction. After this you spend a few weeks with a family, during which you will be mostly on your own. When the trip is over, you meet with the group again and talk about what happened. Sometimes there will be planned get-togethers during the trip.

Some of the programs give you the opportunity to attend school in the country you're visiting. This can be a structured way to meet new people and learn about how the culture works. Because the majority of your trip is spent with a family, and without direct instruction from AFS volunteers, you'll have to act on your own to make it a worthwhile experience. If you're not the type who easily meets new people, or adjusts quickly to a new environment, this may not be the trip for you.

In addition, because the program is almost entirely a homestay, a lot depends on the type of family you end up with. You may find a family that doesn't match your preconceived notions. Many people expect a homestay family to be like the "traditional" American family—a mother, a father, 2.5 kids, and a dog. Just as American families rarely fit this structure, your homestay family might have no kids, lots of kids, or none your age.

The homestay can be a great experience, and many AFSers still keep in touch with their homestay families years after the program is over.

 Melissa Matos of Queens, New York, went with AFS to Italy in the summer before her junior year. She was impressed with the trip: "I met people from all over the world. And I went with an open mind. I wanted to meet the people. I wanted to have a blast over the summer. Then I got to CW Post and I was scared; I didn't know anybody. I started talking to my roommate and everybody just got along right away. Even when we got to Bologna it was awesome. I had a blast in Italy. I want to do it again."

She stayed with a family for four weeks: "We spent a week in language camp, and then a month in the family's house. Then we went to Rome, where we saw everyone again, and we talked to everyone about the negatives and positives of the program. The language instruction was all right. I didn't have any problem with the language."

Matos especially remembers visiting the town festivals: "I went out with my host sister's friend. One day we went out and went swimming and we met a bunch of guys and they took us to the local festivals. The festivals resemble what each town was about. One had a soccer tournament. One had a discotheque. I did a Sfilata, where we modeled wedding dresses from 1980 to 1995. There were twenty of us. We all wore a dress, and then they said something about our dresses."

Although Matos had a great time, she was left mostly to her own devices: "We didn't see the leaders for the entire homestay. They called us to check up, but by the end of the homestay when we met up in Rome, there were new leaders." She thinks that someone who goes should be "willing to learn and to see things. He shouldn't be close-minded about meeting new people. The purpose of this program is to learn a new language and a new culture. I knew this girl whose host sister spoke English. She just hung out with her. She didn't meet anybody. I couldn't understand why she went."

American Trails West

Address 92 Middle Neck Road, Great Neck, NY 11021

Phone (800) 645-6260; (516) 487-2800

Fax (516) 487-2855

E-mail atwtours@aol.com

Cost $4,895–$5,790 (Travel to and from starting point not included.)

Ages 15–18

Size of group 40

Length of program 28–35 days

Application deadline Early applications are preferred. Applications are processed in the order in which they are received.

Description Motorcoach trip to England, France, and Italy.

Summary A great way to see Europe. You will see more of the best sights than by any other means of travel.

History Started in 1965, American Trails West is the largest and perhaps the best of the companies offering student tours. Because of its size, it can offer services and trips that its competitors can't match. And because so many students travel on their trips, they are able to ensure that you hang out with people your own age from all over the country.

The Program An American Trails West tour is probably one of the most pleasurable ways to see Europe with a group. You'll stay in three-star hotels in the major cities, sleep in university residencies in the smaller cities, and camp out for two days. The leaders are efficient and knowledgeable, and the trip is so well planned that you will want for nothing. You will see almost everything that England, France, and Italy have to offer. There's no more comfortable way to see so many European sights in so short a time than by going with American Trails West.

The trip starts in England, where you'll get to explore London, water ski, rock climb, and grass ski. Then it's off across the Channel for ten days in France. You'll tour museums, go dancing in discos, see the great castle of Versailles, and even visit Euro Disney. Then you'll see some ancient towns, stay in a thirteenth-century monastery, and watch thousands of vultures roosting in their cliffside home. Italy is next. You'll spend time in Venice, Florence, and Rome.

Risa Shimizu of Franklin Lakes, New Jersey went with American Trails West on their European Adventures trip. She really enjoyed it: "I had a great time. The staff members are excellent. The people on the trip were great. I made many new friends. The places we went to were really fantastic. I took a history course this year, and everything I saw was memorable. This was probably the most memorable summer I had."

She enjoyed every place that they went, but she was especially excited by Rome: "Rome was the best city. I had a really great time there. Rome is a very metropolitan city, but within the hustle-bustle of the city were ancient ruins. The contrast was really amazing. You were sitting right in the middle of history." She was also impressed with how comfortable the trip was: "The accommodations were very nice; we stayed in three-star and four-star hotels. The food was great."

Shimizu felt that an American Trails West trip is great for almost anyone, but especially for "people who like to travel and see the sights and meet new people. It's not for someone who won't meet new friends. If the people are great, the trip is great. If you're not making the effort to meet new friends, it's not going to work out."

If you go on an ATW European Adventures trip, Shimizu advises that you "be friendly to everybody, because you want to be friends with your companions on the trip. Take in everything that you see and you'll have the most memorable summer that you'll ever have."

Experiment in International Living

Address Kipling Road, P.O. Box 676, Brattleboro, VT 05302

Phone (800) 345-2929; (802) 257-7751

Fax (802) 258-3248

Cost $1,900–$5,000 (Round-trip air fare from NYC, Miami, Boston or LA included, except for trips to Mexico. Financial aid is available. More than one-third of travelers have some type of financial aid.)

Ages Grades 9–12

Size of group 8–18 students with one instructor

Length of programs 3–5 weeks

Application deadline Early applications are preferred. Applications are processed in the order in which they are received. Financial aid is also awarded on a first-come, first-serve basis.

Description A travel program with homestays in Chile, China, Europe, France, Greece, Italy, Mexico, Spain, and Ireland.

Summary The Experiment in International Living is extremely intent on giving you more than a simple tour. They want you to meet the people from an area and become somewhat proficient in communicating with them.

History For more than sixty years, the Experiment in International Living has been providing high school students with extraordinary opportunities for cultural exchange and experience. One of the goals of an Experiment program is the development of international understanding. A participant will complete her trip with a sense that the world is a much smaller place than she thought and that even the most foreign of lands is populated by human beings whose wants, needs, likes, and dislikes are similar to our own.

The Program The Experiment offers such a wide variety of trips and activities that it's difficult to describe a typical program. It's the place to call if you want to go somewhere off the beaten path, and, in that spirit, we will describe its trip to China. Although not

technically a language program, the trip *will* give you an introduction to the Chinese language. What makes the program unique is that you travel with bilingual Chinese students who are able to give you the Chinese perspective on the whole tour.

You start in Chengde, an ancient city in the Yangshan mountains. Then you go to Beijing where you will see Tiananmen Square, the site of the failed 1989 student uprising. In addition, you'll get a chance to see some incredible sights that combine elements of the ancient traditions of China with its new modernization

efforts. While you're traveling, you will participate in daily Chinese lessons. By the end of the trip, you should be able to handle the basic communication skills needed to get around.

Next you'll do a homestay in a Shandong rural village where you can get an idea of what life is like in the Chinese countryside. Your trip ends in Shanghai, where you'll get to visit and explore this wonderful city. Most people leave an Experiment program with a profound understanding and appreciation of another culture.

 Aaron Jusino of the Bronx, New York went with the Experiment to Italy when he was seventeen. He loved it: "It was the best experience I had in my whole entire life. It was so intense; it was incredible. The best part about it was being out there and getting a sense of independence. Not many people give young kids a chance to be on their own, especially in another country."

Jusino's favorite part of the trip was his homestay. He stayed with a family for three weeks and developed a tight relationship with them. "We did so many things together. We went motorbike riding. We went to the beach. They threw a birthday party for me. After that we went to a club; they provided transportation. We stayed up in the living room and talked to three or four in the morning sometimes."

Jusino remembers one night especially fondly: "On the fourth of July, my host family took me to the store and we bought fireworks. We were running through the fields setting off fireworks left and right. It was really amazing. After that, we came home and sat on the terrace. My host mother was playing the guitar and we were singing songs. Than night I taught them how to do the "Time Warp" from the "Rocky Horror Picture Show." It was so funny. It was hysterical. We were listening to "Rocky Horror" all night. They were really into it. It was two o'clock in the morning, and we were all dancing."

He also really liked his counselors: "I loved the counselors. Our counselor was really supportive. I got a stomachache. She was really supportive, buying me chamomile tea. 'Oh please don't die on me.' When I thought I lost my wallet, she took me to the police and helped me. But it was at home all the time."

An Experiment trip isn't for everyone, however; you have to be outgoing. "Shy, bashful people don't learn that much. There were two shy girls who hung out together but didn't do anything. They didn't have a good time. They didn't get the concept of the whole trip."

One of Experiment's guiding philosophies is that the unexpected is better than the planned: "They told us that the best part is getting lost. It's more of an adventure when you get lost. You can learn a lot more. I got lost for five hours in Venice. I saw little museums and streets I wouldn't have seen otherwise. The different things I encountered were great."

Interlocken—Crossroads Student Travel

Address Interlocken RR2 Box 165, Hillsboro, NH 03244

Phone (603) 478-3166

Fax (603) 478-5260

Cost $3,280–$4,330 (Travel to and from starting point not included.)

Ages grades 9–12

Size of group 12–15 students with 2 leaders

Length of program 28–42 days

Application deadline Early applications are preferred. Applications are processed in the order in which they are received.

Description Photojournalism trips to China and Berlin. Environment/World Change trips to Alaska, the Caribbean, and Israel. Language trips to Japan and France.

Summary On the photojournalism trips, in addition to visiting a foreign land, you'll get to improve your writing, thinking, and artistic skills. The environmental trips will increase your awareness of the complex environmental situation in the world.

History Started in 1967 by Interlocken (an international summer camp), Crossroads Student tours give you the chance to engage in cross-cultural exploration and physical challenges. They attempt to make cultural exploration an adventure and a learning experience.

The Program Although not a foreign country, Alaska is so far away from the contiguous forty-eight states that it can feel like one. With everything you need on your back, you'll trek through some of the wildest parts of the state. During the trip, your leaders will discuss the different environmental issues concerning the places you are visiting. For example, when you explore the islands near the Southeast's Inland Passage, you'll study the habitat and habits of bears, learn about the logging industry, and gain insights about aboriginal cultures. By the time the trip is over, you will not only have met formidable physical challenges, you will have acquired a better understanding of how governments have to balance environmental conservation with attempts to fulfill the immense material requirements of modern populations.

Crossroads' two photojournalism trips offer you excellent opportunities to improve your writing and artistic skills, and to learn a great deal about different cultures. By encouraging you to set up links to your local or school newspapers, Crossroads can also help you on your way to getting published. For four to six weeks, you can be a foreign journalist exploring the lands of Germany or China, seeking interesting stories and images that you won't find back home. Your guides will help you find and write stories, and the best of your work will appear in a newspaper published by Crossroads. Not only are these trips great learning experiences, but they also give you valuable practice if you are planning a career in journalism.

James Barnes of Seattle, Washington went with Interlocken to Israel: "It was absolutely excellent. One of the cool things was we did several different homestays with different families.

"We worked on a kibbutz for ten days, and we were getting up at 5:30 in the morning and shoveling two-meter ditches in the sand. We were working for our lodging and food. We also got to spend a lot of time with the kibbutz kids our ages. We did dances at night and kind of exchanges of culture.

"We stayed in a Moshav, a more modern kibbutz. It's the same type of idea, but instead of 100 percent going to the kibbutz, they got to keep their own salary. They ate in their own houses instead of a kibbutz. It's more modern. Less socialism. There we stayed with families and got to know them, which was awesome. There wasn't a language barrier. Everyone speaks English.

"Then later we stayed with Arab families. We were getting the full perspective. From doing Shabbat Friday night to witnessing the Arabs doing their Muslim prayers, and eating different foods."

At the end of the trip, the group went on a camel trip through the Negev desert. Barnes especially remembers his Bedouin guide: "Our Bedouin guide was named Shimon and he had an interesting philosophy of life that made me think about a lot of things. He never was interested in knowing specifically what time it was. He talked in a very soft voice, and he was really into his surrounding environment. He was always giving us geology lessons about the layers of rocks in the Sinai desert. He was really upset with the modern world, especially about how it was too narrow, always living in the future or the past but never paying attention to the present. He had this acute awareness of what was going on around him and enjoying the moment. And this attitude translated into everything he did because he was living off the land. Getting hit with a new perspective has really changed me. It has made me slow down and smell the flowers."

Barnes' advice for anyone going on a trip like this is to "always keep a positive and open mind even when the viewpoint and perspective that you're seeing is totally the opposite from what you're used to. You have to be sensitive to the fact that you're in someone else's country and not your own. You have to respect their ways."

Putney Student Travel

Address P.O. Box 707, Putney, VT 05346

Phone (802) 387-5885

Fax (802) 387-4276

Cost $6,290–$7,490 (includes round-trip airfare from NYC or LA. Limited financial aid is available based on need.)

Ages For students completing grades 8–12

Size of group 16–18 people per group with 2 leaders

Length of programs 35–40 days

Application deadline Early applications are preferred. Applications are processed in the order in which they are received.

Description Trips to Europe, Australia, and China.

Summary Trips are meant to avoid touristy areas and to give you an indoctrination into the cultures of the countries visited. Most include a short homestay, and take you off the beaten path.

History Founded in 1952, Putney Student Travel offers a range of programs for high school students. They offer a learning experience that is fostered by doing and not by watching. A good Putney trip requires participants who are willing to take care of themselves. If you're eager to try new things, you will have an experience that you will remember for the rest of your life.

The Program Putney's travel programs are notable for their emphasis on doing things that the normal tourist might not. Whether it's gathering with Italian villagers in the village square to tell stories, or traveling the roads of rural China by bike, you will experience aspects of the country you visit that would be difficult to find on your own. To give you an idea of the range of activities on a typical Putney trip, we're going to describe a trip they call *Plan 2: Australia, New Zealand, and Fiji.* You'll start by flying from LA to tropical Cairns near the Great Barrier Reef on the coast of Australia. There you'll mountain bike for five days through North Queensland. Part of the bike trip will be through the tropical rain forest where you might see emus (one of the biggest and fastest birds you'll probably ever come across) and kangaroos.

Next, you will spend a week on a forty-foot yacht where you'll get to snorkel in the crystal-clear waters over the Reef. The Great Barrier Reef, the largest natural structure in the world (1,250 miles long, to be exact) is home to hordes of amazing sea creatures that will truly blow you away. After the reef, it's off to Sydney for five days of cosmopolitan variety, Australian-style.

Your next stop is New Zealand, where you'll live with a local family for a week. After a few days of skiing in the New Zealand Alps, it's off to Fiji, where you'll finish the program on a magnificent beach. A trip with Putney will be one that will leave you with stories to tell for years.

 Stephanie Ayers from Corpus Christi, Texas went with Putney on its Plan I trip to Switzerland, Italy, France, and Holland. She found the experience exhilarating, and was amazed at both the amount she learned about Europe and the great things that she saw. But the trip "was more of a learning experience of people than of facts. The people on the trip were mostly from the Northeast. I was the only one from the remote South . . . There were eighteen students. You meet seventeen new people who are going to be your family for the next six weeks. You have to get to know them."

The high point of the trip (in more ways than one) for Ayers was rock climbing in the Dolomite mountains of Italy. "You had a belay partner. You're tied together with a bunch of cords, and you help each other get up the mountain, both morally and physically. We were climbing up these vertical rocks. Oh my gosh. It was so scary."

Also in Italy, Ayers got to spend five days with a family. Although she didn't speak Italian and the parents of the family didn't speak English, communication was still possible because of a daughter who showed Ayers around, and introduced her to her friends. "The daughter made me feel comfortable. I felt comfortable around friends. They all studied English. We shared stories about our countries." Ayers made special note about the quality of the leaders: "They were great," she said. And they were good at encouraging the participants to try new things and to explore the area.

The trip, however, was not for everybody. "You need to feel comfortable with new people" and you have to have spent some time outside. "There was one girl who didn't know how to ride a bike. I couldn't figure out why she was on the tour." To get the most out of the trip, you should "take advantage of everything you can and every opportunity you get. Even if you're tired, do it anyway. It will be worth it later on."

Rotary International

Address 1560 Sherman Ave., Evanston, IL 60201-3698

Phone (800) 423-6418; (708) 866-3000

Costs $1,495-$2,995 (Includes travel costs and all insurance costs. Most applicants must complete the exchange process by either hosting a foreign student or locating a host family.)

Ages 14-22

Size of group 15-40

Lengths of programs 3- 8 weeks

Application deadline April 30; the most popular programs fill up quickly.

Description Short motorcoach trips and homestay programs in Argentina, Australia, Belgium, Brazil, Colombia, England, Finland, France, Germany, Holland, Israel, Italy, Japan, Mexico, Norway, Spain, South Africa, Sweden, and Switzerland.

Summary An excellent, inexpensive way to learn about the world. Students are set up with homestay families who take responsibility for most activities. A local Rotary representative helps make sure things are running well.

History Rotary has been sponsoring Student Exchange programs for over thirty years. An organization of business and professional leaders from all over the world, Rotary believes in promoting ethical standards in business and in promoting world understanding and peace through programs like the youth exchange.

The Program Because the Rotary program is so decentralized, the way your trip is organized and priced will depend on where you apply. Each Rotary club or district sponsors kids to go on the programs. You pay for travel and insurance, and they cover everything else. To go on one of these exchange programs, you must apply at the local level, and depending on where you apply, the process can be competitive: you will have to fill out a written application and go through a personal interview. If you do succeed, however, you'll be able to go on an exchange program for little more than the price of travel.

Just like any homestay program, a Rotary program requires a great deal of maturity. You'll be living in someone else's home, and while this will give you a great view of life in another country, it isn't just a quick visit. Just as you have to get along with the people in your own home, you will have to find common ground with your host family. You may get along great with everyone, but you also may run into the same conflicts you might find in your own home. Just don't forget, you *are* a guest.

In addition, although you will have contact with local Rotarians in whatever country you're visiting, you won't be spending much time with Americans. A Rotary program is about total immersion in another culture. This will leave you with a memorable experience, but it can also leave you homesick.

If you do go on a program, you'll most likely be required to serve as a host for someone from the country your visiting. Being a host family can be a challenge, but the potential rewards are great. You will make lasting ties with both your homestay family and the person who stays with your family. These ties can allow the experience to continue for many years after the program ends.

 David Kutch of Pineville, Louisiana went to Hungary with the help of his local Rotary club. He learned a great deal about the Hungarian people and how their culture was changing. He was especially happy with his homestay family: "They were so eager to help me. My family was great. They were just basically mellowed-out. If they would have been in the United States for Woodstock, they would have been there."

Kutch, who is fascinated by the original Woodstock, got the chance to see Canned Heat (a band who had played there) in Hungary: "It was awesome to hear them play. The Hungarians couldn't understand what the band was saying, but the music made up for it. I heard a lot of rock and roll over there; my family was into music, and they took me to see a lot."

The Rotary club usually requires that you serve as a host family in return for your hospitality. "I brought my host sister back. It was interesting. She was really outgoing and wanted to do everything. She wanted to see so many things, but we were surprised at what she liked the most. She went wild when she saw her first mall."

"There's not much to see in Pineville, so we took her to New Orleans, and showed her the sights. We had her try Cajun food, and showed her the aquarium. She was glowing from ear to ear the whole time she was here."

If you do go on a Rotary club trip, Kutch advises that you "get as much information as you can, and go for it. It's an experience you're going to remember for your lifetime."

LANGUAGE PROGRAMS

If you speak a foreign language and want to get better at it this summer, the best way is to spend some time immersed in the culture where the language is spoken. Although you can get a sense of how a foreign language works through lessons at school, you will never get good enough to use the language unless you're in a situation that forces you to speak it, and there are intensive classes available that will do just that. With that in mind, there are many programs that offer intensive language schooling in a country where that language is spoken. You will be immersed in the culture, most likely living with a family that does not speak English.

Besides gaining proficiency in your chosen language, you'll also experience another country in a more complete way than you could ever imagine. Although a tour through France, for example, can be phenomenal—it *is* beautiful—you will be amazed at how much more you experience the country when you speak French as well. You will meet French people and be able to converse with them, and find out their viewpoint of the world and see if it differs much from your own.

The homestay that is included in many of these programs is also an experience that should not be missed. From the time that you spend with your host family, you will not only develop essential language skills, but you will gain another family. Many home-stay participants keep in touch with their families for many years after they go to a country. We know of some who have actually served as home-stay hosts for the grandchildren of the families they originally stayed with.

Of course, you may not have studied a language in school. It's not too late (actually, it's never too late). Many of these programs will accept students who have only one year of a language, or who have not studied a language at all. But most likely, you will have a more complete experience if you have started studying the language, or if you plan to continue it after the trip. If you do decide on one of these trips, try to find a way to begin learning the language as soon as possible. It will be much easier if you get started before the trip begins.

AFS (American Field Service)

Address 220 East 42nd Street, 3rd floor, New York, NY 10017

Phone (800) AFS-INFO; (212) 949-4242

Cost $2,895–$3,595 (Round-trip airfare from NYC, Miami, or LA included.)

Ages 14–17

Size of group 5–60 (depending on the location)

Length of programs 28–45 days

Application deadline April 15

Description Language programs in Argentina, Belgium-France, Canada, Chile, Costa Rica, France, Germany, Japan, Russia, Venezuela.

Summary A challenging language program that requires a good deal of responsibility. You may face many of the challenges on your own.

History AFS is one of the oldest and largest travel programs in the country. It offers some of the longest homestays in the business, and expects a great deal of responsibility from its participants. You will, without a doubt, learn a great deal about the day-to-day life and culture of the place you're visiting.

The Program Just like their homestay programs (see pages 179–180), the AFS language programs are focused on a stay with a host family. You will fly with other AFS participants to a big city in the country you're visiting. There you'll be introduced to the host family with whom you'll be staying for the bulk of the trip. While the amount of language study varies depending on the program (in Costa Rica, you get twelve hours a week; in Japan twenty), you will always have plenty of time to explore the country in which you're living.

Some of the programs allow you to attend a local high school while you're learning. This is a great way to improve your language skills and glean singular insight into another country's customs.

At the end of the program, you'll meet up with AFS volunteers and discuss what happened. Just like the AFS homestay programs, however, you will be mainly on your own. AFS programs are an excellent way to meet people in a foreign land. You will be forced to meet people who don't speak English, and your language skills will improve immensely.

 Marie Boucher of Wilton, Connecticut spent the summer before her junior year in Japan with an AFS program. She learned a lot: "I was there for three months over the summer. I spent most of the time in a small town outside of Osaka with a family—a husband and a wife and three dogs.

"Half of the time, I spent commuting into the city to go to school everyday. It was a lab set up by Sony to teach English-speaking people to speak Japanese. The instruction was intense. By the time I was out four weeks later, I could really carry on a conversation.

"The family was good. I got along really well with my host father. It was lucky that I even got to go to Japan. AFS told me that they had no more rooms for girls in their homestay program, so I had to switch to the language programs. It was a little more expensive, but I'm glad I did it. This family asked specifically for a girl. My host father told me 'Boys smell.'"

Boucher specifically remembers getting lost in the Osaka train station: "They have these huge train stations. The main one in Osaka has this huge mall around it. It's got three floors below and about seven stories above. One day, I was looking for a music store on one of the floors. I got lost looking for it. For four or five hours I was looking for it in the mall. I would go up an escalator to a place I thought I knew. While I was lost, I came across a huge TV screen. It just happened to be during the O. J. Simpson chase

scene, and all these Japanese people were looking confusedly at the TV screen because it was CNN, and they couldn't figure out what was going on."

Boucher feels that most people can gain from a trip like this. If you "can take care of yourself or can learn to take care of yourself, you'll have a good time. I went being really calm and meek and I returned very assertive. A friend lost her ticket on the way back. I went to the woman at the counter and demanded that she give my friend a ticket and she did. I wouldn't have done that before. I come from a school that is very sheltered. I think a lot of people can learn how to assert themselves."

If you do go to Japan, Boucher advises that you "learn how to use the toilet. There are three kinds. Don't be afraid, it's not going to bite. Also, even if something doesn't appeal to you, make sure you try it. Don't be afraid to make a fool of yourself. You have to learn how to try new things whether you want to or not. Sometimes you'll surprise yourself."

Academic Studies Associates

Address 355 Main Street, P.O. Box 800, Armonk, NY 10504-0800

Phone (800) 752-2250; (914) 273-2250

Fax (914) 273-5430

Costs $3,695-$4,095 (Travel to and from starting point not included.)

Ages Students finishing grades 10–12

Size of classes 8 students

Size of program 60–75 students

Length of program 28–35 days

Application deadline Early applications are preferred. Applications are processed in the order in which they are received.

Prerequisites Students must have studied at least one and sometimes two years of either French or Spanish

Description An intensive, all-encompassing language program in France, and Spain. You will speak only French or Spanish for the entire trip.

Summary A challenging and fun language program that includes intensive personalized study, a homestay, and elective classes on different French/Spanish subjects (taught in French or Spanish). Two types of programs are offered an intensive homestay program and an on-campus program.

Special options Tennis programs: $295–$495

History Since 1983, ASA has been running pre-college enrichment programs in Oxford for high school students. This experience has proven valuable in the establishment of their language programs in France, and Spain.

The Program ASA's language programs offer two different approaches. One is a homestay program; you will be totally immersed in either a French or Spanish-speaking environment. You will spend your mornings studying the language and your evenings practicing it. Your instructors will insist that you not speak English during the trip, and by the time you get done, you will be dreaming in your chosen language. The other type of program is a residential, on-campus program. You'll be living on a campus in Spain or France studying Spanish, French, and a few electives relevant to the country you're visiting. Living on-campus, you'll spend more time around other Americans than you would living with a host family, and the program may not be as intense.

This is not necessarily a bad thing. It's sometimes uncomfortable to try to live in another family's home, to follow their customs, to eat their food. By staying on a campus with other Americans, you can still work hard at improving your language skills and learning about the culture of another country.

With this in mind, we are going to describe the ASA program at the University of Nice in France. In this program, you'll live in a university residence hall. There you'll have a great view of the city and still be within a ten-minute walk of the beach.

You will study French every day for three and a half hours. The language classes are intense, but you'll get plenty of time to practice your newly learned French while exploring Nice. In addition to the classes, the program offers excursions to great museums and picturesque villages within the region.

The classes are not devoted to language alone. In the evenings, you'll be able to take several classes on aspects of French culture such as French civilization or art history. For an additional $140, you can take a class in French cooking as well.

By the time you finish the language program, your French will have improved, and you'll have a better sense of what life is like in France.

Shane Glass of Los Angeles, California went with ASA to Spain the summer before his junior year and then again the summer before his senior year: "I thought it was fun, relaxing, and an overall good time. I went to the beach for hours every day. I went out to clubs at night, and I stayed with a Spanish family."

The coolest thing he saw was a bullfight: "First all the bullfighters come out and show themselves. Then they send one bull out to run around. A man pokes the bull in the neck to make him weaker, and somebody throws spears at the bull to make it look good. The matador kills the bull and throws the ear to the audience. The crowd loves it, but you feel sorry for the bull. If the matador doesn't kill the bull, he goes to jail. Seeing it in real life was different from seeing it on TV."

The ASA program would be good for "anyone who wants to have a good time and improve his Spanish." If you go, Glass advises that you "hang out mostly with the Spanish kids. That's where your Spanish improves."

Experiment in International Living

Address Kipling Road, P.O. Box 676, Brattleboro, VT 05302

Phone (800) 345-2929; (802)257-7751

Fax (802) 258-3248

Cost $1,900–$5,000 (Round-trip airfare from NYC included, except for trips to Mexico. Financial aid is available. More than one-third of travelers receive some type of financial aid.)

Ages 14–18

Size of group 8–18 students with one instructor

Length of program 3–5 weeks

Application deadline Early applications are preferred. Applications are processed in the order in which they are received. Financial aid is also awarded on a first-come, first-serve basis.

Description A language program with homestays in Costa Rica, France, Japan, Mexico, and Spain.

Summary The Experiment in International Living's language programs will give you more than just language instruction; they'll give you insight into another culture.

History For more than sixty years, the Experiment in International Living has been providing high school students with extraordinary opportunities for international exchange and experience. They believe an effective language program requires cultural immersion.

The Program All of the Experiment's language programs are centered on an extended homestay where you get to practice your language skills. The trip to Mexico is no exception. You'll start with a three-day orientation in Mexico City. Then it's off to Oaxaca where you'll spend four weeks living with a host family.

You'll study Spanish on weekdays from 9 A.M. to 1 P.M. in small groups arranged by ability. Then in the afternoons, you'll get to practice your conversations in the markets and with your host family. Because you're in a situation where you must use your language skills to communicate, you'll be forced to improve. By the end of the program, you will be amazed at how easily you can communicate with your new friends and family.

 Catelin Mathers-Suter went with Experiment to France. Although you will learn a lot of French on the Experiment's program, French is not all that it was about. Mathers-Suter spent three weeks with a family and also had plenty of opportunity to practice her language in everyday life: "We were living with French families that spoke very little English. There was a lot of Franglais. I swear the only way I learned French was because I was living with a family."

The leaders in an Experiment program try to teach people to communicate in more than just words. They also believe in a degree of freedom that is rare among the other programs mentioned in this book. At one point, Mathers-Suter and a friend were late coming back to a meeting place to return to the hotel. They were left a note with some money, and were told to find their own way back. "So we decided to go out, just two girls in Paris. We got lost, and for two hours were trying to find our way back to the hotel. I remember us being in an alleyway with all these French men hitting on us. They had no intentions of doing anything, but we had no idea. We didn't understand the cultural differences and we were so scared about getting home. We finally figured out how to use the telecard. [In many places in Europe, pay phones don't accept coins. They accept these disposable phone cards.] We didn't have the hotel's number and we had to find out how to get back. We called the Experiment's office, but the person who answered didn't speak English. We had to use French to get back. You were forced to use French, and that's how you learn."

Of course everything worked out for the best. These students got an unforgettable experience and were able to learn more than just how to speak French. They learned how to communicate. To go on one of these programs, you need to be "able to be away from home. You have to be able to open your mind and accept another person's culture. Even though it's just France in Europe, the culture differences were huge. You have to want to learn."

If you do go, Mathers-Suter advises that you shouldn't "be afraid to speak the language. When they're laughing they're not laughing at you, just at the fact that you're trying to speak the language." An Experiment program is not for everyone. But if you feel you can get beyond the initial frustration you might feel trying to communicate, it is an excellent program for a cross-cultural adventure.

Putney Student Travel

Address P.O. Box 707, Putney, VT 05346

Phone (802) 387-5885

Fax (802) 387-4276

Cost $5,090–$6,290 (Round-trip airfare from NYC or LA included.)

Ages 12–18 (Participants for the more popular trips are grouped by age. Limited financial aid is available based on need.)

Size of group 16–18 people per group with 2 leaders

Length of program 33–40 days

Application deadline Early applications are preferred. Applications are processed in the order in which they are received.

Description Intense language instruction in France and Spain.

Summary Putney believes that total immersion in a foreign language will give students improved language ability. Their language programs require that students speak the language throughout the program. Participants must be mature and willing to make mistakes.

History Founded in 1952, Putney Student Travel offers a range of programs for high school students. Each program presents a learning experience that is fostered by doing and not by watching. A good Putney trip requires participants who are willing to take care of themselves and be responsible for their own learning. If you're willing to try new things, you will have an amazing experience that you will remember for the rest of your life.

The Program Even if you've never enjoyed learning a language in school, it's a whole different experience the Putney way. Putney believes that language cannot be learned in a vacuum, that the only way to become good at a language is to use it to communicate. Because you will be living your life in French or Spanish on the trip, you will reach a fluency that you didn't believe possible and you may even start dreaming in your chosen language. The language instruction is geared to each individual; the goal, to improve as much as possible.

Putney's *Plan V* in France is an excellent example of their approach to language learning. You'll begin in the château country of the Loire valley. You'll need your language skills to converse with the shopkeepers and the French students you meet during your trip. Then it's off to Brittany where you'll spend a week in a rural fishing village. You'll be required to join in some aspect of the life of the town, and then report on your experience orally in French. After that, you get a week in Paris to sight-see and explore.

All this study and practice comes in handy when you begin your homestay in a small town like Annecy. You'll have to communicate with your family, and, in addition to picking up language skills, you may even make friends that you'll keep for life. Then it's off to Provence and then south to the Riviera to see some of the most popular beaches in the world. The trip ends in the French Alps, where you'll get to hike, rock climb, or ski. By the time you head home, you will be amazed at how much your skills have improved.

 Lisa Ludwig, who went on Putney's Plan XI trip to France, felt that the trip was a "great experience. Kind of right from the beginning, they made you feel really comfortable. We flew into Paris, and then went to Loire valley. All the people on the trip were great to be with. The counselors were young. They were both excellent at French. Everything ran really smoothly."

The language part of the program is intensive. "We had to speak French at all times, even when we talked with each other, but when the counselors weren't looking, we went off that some." Even the counselors might speak English to get an important point across. "When they did we knew we were

in trouble," said Ludwig. The program only had one week of formal French lessons, but because the participants spoke French most of the time, everyone improved. Ludwig notes that "By the end I felt pretty good about my French. I could actually carry on a conversation with a French-speaking person."

Ludwig's advice for anyone going on the trip is to pack lightly: "Don't bring a lot of clothes. I brought way, way too much. You'll be sitting in the heat thinking, 'Why did I bring so much stuff.'" She ended up sending home a suitcase so she wouldn't have to carry it along.

Rassias Language Programs Abroad

Address P.O. Box 5456, Hanover, NH 03755

Phone (800) 544-3216; (603) 643-3007

Fax (603) 643-4249

Cost $4,650–$5,730 (Round-trip airfare from NYC included.)

Ages 14–16

Size of group 15–18 people per group with 3 staff members

Length of program 31–36 days

Application deadline Early applications are preferred. Applications are processed in the order in which they are received. Final deadline is April 30.

Description Language instruction in Spanish or French. Features a homestay. Participant must have studied at least one and sometimes two years of either French or Spanish to participate in a trip.

Summary A good program for boning up on your French or Spanish and getting to know the people from two great European cultures. The excellent language instruction is only part of an intense learning experience.

History Rassias Language programs, started ten years ago by Helene Rassias, aims to give students an intense and intimate look at French or Spanish culture. Using the Rassias Method® of language instruction, the instruc-

tors believe that a language cannot be separated from its surrounding cultures. When you travel with Rassias, you will be living, breathing, and eating French or Spanish culture.

The Program The highlight of any Rassias trip is the homestay. Because you will stay with actual families, you will get an insight into the essential nature of the culture that you're visiting. On the *France "A" program,* you will start in the Loire Valley, with orientation. Here group leaders will discuss with you what cultural differences you can expect when you go out to meet your family.

After a few days of orientation, you will move in with your host family. Your days will be spent studying French in class, your evenings and weekends at home with your family practicing what you have learned.

The next step is a trip to Brittany, a beautiful and popular French vacation spot. As with all the Rassias programs, this one stays away from tourist traps. You will meet French people on this trip, and you will have to speak French. Finally after a short stop in historic Normandy (where Allied forces landed on D-day in World War II), it's off to Paris. By the time you finish the trip, you will have developed outstanding language skills and had an experience that you will not soon forget.

 The Rassias Language Program requires a serious commitment to learning and communicating in French. Melissa Lem, who went on their "B" program, found the language instruction exceptional, with lots of drills that ended up being useful during the trip. "It was pretty intense. The drills and school. I was in French Four, with four years of French, but I learned a great deal. My French totally improved. My ear was a lot better."

During the first week of orientation, her group slept in a youth hostel and hiked in the Pyrenees. Then they went to Arles for a homestay. The homestay was the best part. "I got a good family. I had an older sister and a younger brother. They were so nice to me," says Lem, who wishes the homestay part of the trip had been longer. She still keeps in touch with her family. "They sent me a Christmas gift, and my French sister writes to me."

Lem, who was seventeen at the time of the trip and who lives in New York City, did find the supervision a bit too strict. "When we were in Paris, they didn't let us out of the compound alone. This was a little lame." On the other hand, Paris is a big city, and for some of those coming from small-town suburban America, this supervision might be welcome.

Lem's advice for anyone going on the trip is to "make the most out of your homestay" and also be willing to experience new things. "You have to be open to being with new people, eating new food, living in crappy conditions."

COMMUNITY SERVICE PROGRAMS

Let's say you decide that you'd like to travel, to see the world, but you would also like to give something back at the same time. It turns out that there are programs that allow you to do just that. You get to travel somewhere and help people less fortunate than yourself.

Lend a Hand

In most of these programs, you'll be required to put in a lot of hard work in an impoverished area. You'll help build roads, or plant crops, or clean up garbage. The great thing about these programs is that you get to be actively involved in the lives of the people you meet. You *can* make a difference.

Paying to Make a Difference

These trips are not cheap, however. They're less expensive than traditional travel programs, but you will still be paying for the privilege of giving. If you think about it, this makes sense. Your travel and living expenses have to be paid by somebody, and that somebody is you.

This is not to say that if you can't afford one of these trips, you can't do community service. There are many opportunities within your own neighborhood that don't cost a penny. While you won't get the experience of traveling to an isolated village somewhere (unless, that is, you live in an isolated village somewhere), you will still get the same satisfaction of having done a good deed that those who travel half-way around the world get. If you want to take part in community service in your own hometown, see pages 39-41 for more information.

Experiment in International Living

Address Kipling Road, P.O. Box 676, Brattleboro, VT 05302

Phone (800) 345-2929; (802) 257-7751

Fax (802) 258-3248

Cost $2,900–$5,000 (Round-trip air fare from NYC, Miami, or LA included. Financial aid is available. More than one-third of travelers receive some type of financial aid.)

Ages 14–17

Size of group 8–18 students with one instructor

Length of program 3–5 weeks

Application deadline Early applications are preferred. Applications are processed in the order in which they are received. Financial aid is also awarded on a first-come, first-serve basis.

Description The Experiment's community service programs are located in Ghana, Kenya, and Mexico. It has ecological adventure programs in Australia, Belize, and Ecuador.

Summary The Experiment in International Living's Community Service and ecological programs feature homestays and give you insight into the ecological problems this organization deals with.

History For more than sixty years, the Experiment in International Living has been providing high school students with extraordinary opportunities for cultural exchange and experience. They believe a community service program should include immersion in the culture of the people that you're trying to help.

The Program The Experiment's ecological adventure program in Ecuador, while not a typical community service program, will give you a sense of how their programs work. You begin by spending a few days in Quito, the ancient capital of Ecuador. There you will have a chance to explore the beautiful baroque churches while you undergo orientation. You will learn about Ecuador's amazing geographic diversity and about the famous Galapagos Islands.

After the stay in Quito, you'll go on a three-week homestay with a family nearby. You'll get to know your family and spend time exploring the local area. The ecological part of the trip reaches its head when you travel to the Galapagos Islands. The inspiration for Darwin's revolutionary theory of evolution, the Galapagos Islands have been threatened by the enormous number of tourists they attract. You will explore the islands and discuss ways in which to protect their fragile ecosystems.

The last night of the trip will be spent reflecting on the things that you have learned. You will find that you have a much greater appreciation of global environmental problems, and of the complex interrelations between the economy and the environment.

 Erin Genia of South Salem, New York went with the Experiment to Belize. "It was really great. I learned a lot—an infinite amount. Just being in a different culture itself was a great experience."

She particularly liked the homestay: "The homestay was great. It was difficult for me to adjust. It was a family with ten children. I'm used to living in totally different conditions, having my own room, and having privacy."

She especially remembers one village festival: "One time when we were in the village, they were having a festival. There was music, and people were playing games. We were sitting around observing; some of us were playing Frisbee, and I was around a bunch of kids. There was this gigantic bug. Really, really big. Three inches long and big. Big. Really big. These kids just picked it up and were playing with it and naturally I was afraid of it. It had pinchers. Really big ones. Really big. It was a really big bug. And so I didn't want to be near it, so I started to walk away. The children noticed that I didn't want to be near it and started taunting me, putting it on my shoulder and my back. It would climb up and it was horrible. Horrible!

"I left the scene. I started running, but the children followed me with the bug, running after me. Everybody was standing around. Nobody would help me. It was horrible, but it was really funny. But now I'm no longer afraid of big bugs."

If you do go on the trip, Genia advises that you shouldn't "jump to conclusions. Be as open-minded as you can, and be ready."

Interlocken—Global Routes

Address Interlocken RR2 Box 165, Hillsboro, NH 03244

Phone (603) 478-3166

Fax (603) 478-5260

Cost $2,590–$3,790 (Travel to and from starting point not included. Global Routes requires that you raise around $300 to help buy supplies for the projects of the trip. A percentage of the cost of the trip might be tax deductible.)

Ages 14–18

Size of group 18 students with 2 leaders and 2 local staff members

Length of program 28–49 days

Application deadline Early applications are preferred. Applications are processed in the order in which they are received.

Description Community service trips to Navajo tribe, Arapho tribe, Brazil, Ecuador, Costa Rica, Belize, Thailand, Nepal, Zimbabwe, and Kenya

Summary Community service programs that require a commitment of time and energy to solve problems in poor areas. Requires maturity and a willingness to deal with unplanned events.

History A nonprofit organization affiliated with Interlocken (an international summer camp), Global Routes Community Service gives you a chance to live like a Peace Corps volunteer and help improve life in small, third-

world villages. They believe that by helping people, you can learn about yourself as well.

The Program Because of the varied locations of the different Global Route travel programs, the locale and people that you encounter in one program will differ substantially from those in another. However, they all involve some type of physical labor and living with the people that you're helping. The program in Thailand starts with an orientation in Kancahanaburi. There you will learn some basic Thai and some of the history and culture of Thailand. Although knowing Thai might be helpful on the trip, many Thai people speak English, so you'll still get to meet people without knowing the language.

Then it's off to the village where you'll live and build a one-room school house. You'll start from scratch, buying timber and setting up the foundation, and continue until you're hanging the blackboards. During the building process, you'll be living with families whose simple lifestyle is probably radically different from your own. When you're not building the school, you'll be teaching English to students in the area.

After the school is built, you'll hike, ride elephants, and travel by raft on a river winding through the hills. (Yes, we did say elephant.) After this adventure, you'll get to explore the city of Bangkok for two days and then go to an island in the Gulf of Thailand, where you can hang out on the beach and relax before you go home.

A trip like this can be an eye-opener, showing you the vast differences and remarkable similarities that exist among different areas of the world. Most people are amazed at how much they grow on a trip like this, but it does take a certain amount of responsibility to accept the fact that not all of the world is like America.

Marni Richman went on Global Route's five-week trip to Costa Rica. The trip actually started a few weeks earlier when she raised money. "I wrote an involved letter about why I was doing this to my parents' friends. During the stay, I sent postcards, and after the stay, I showed them before and after pictures of the work that we had done. I think it's nice that we had to raise money." The participants could see how the money was spent.

Richman arrived in Costa Rica, where she and the group stayed in a youth hostel for a few days to get oriented. After this, they spent two-and-a-half weeks with a family and built a playground. "The playground was pretty much as hard as you wanted it to be. It was a lot of mixing concrete and putting in the actual structure. You didn't have to work hard. But we all did. You were there to work. The townspeople actually came out to help you. When you saw the kids playing with it, all the hard work was worth it."

After building the playground they went to a rainforest and helped build trails. According to Richman "the work in the rain forest was the hardest work that I have ever done. We walked straight uphill half an hour to get there. Then we carried fifteen-pound bags of sand and made trails." But because the location was so beautiful, the work was almost fun.

Richman's advice to anyone going on the program is to "be prepared to live a really different lifestyle. When you're living in a third-world country, things are different and slower. You're not always in a nice house with a nice shower and a toilet that flushes." Richman's trip was well organized and fulfilling. She highly recommends Global Routes to anyone looking for a community service program.

Putney Student Travel—Seeds for Progress

Address Putney, VT 05346

Phone (802) 387-5885

Fax (802) 387-4276

E-mail pst@sover.net

Cost $3,290–$5,590 (Round-trip airfare from NYC or LA included, except for U.S. trips. Limited financial aid is available based on need.)

Ages 14–18 (Participants for the more popular trips are grouped by age.)

Size of group 16–18 people per group with 2 leaders

Length of program 27–31 days

Application deadline Early applications are preferred. Applications are processed in the order in which they are received.

Description Community service programs in the West Indies, Tanzania, the Czech Republic, Costa Rica, Ecuador, Montana, and Vermont.

Summary Putney's Community Service programs send you to a poor area that has requested aid, and involve you in various construction projects. The experience is enriching. You will leave with a strong sense of the value of helping people and a better understanding of who you are.

History Since 1952, Putney Student Travel has offered a range of programs for high school students. On their trips, you learn by doing and not by watching. A good Putney trip

requires participants who are willing to take care of themselves and be responsible for their own learning. If you're game and willing to try new things, you will have an amazing experience that you will remember for the rest of your life.

The Program Putney changes the nature of its service programs fairly often in response to the needs of the communities in which they work. So any program we describe may be substantially different from the one that you travel on. One of Putney's Seeds for Progress's newest programs is that in the Czech Republic. You will spend thirty days in the Czech Federal Republic helping in the slow transition from the Communist policies of the cold war period. In 1993, Czechoslovakia dissolved into two independent republics, but the damage done by years of Soviet domination has yet to be repaired. You will go to the Czech Federal Republic to help on one of a number of projects.

The great thing about the program is that you'll be working along with Czech students eager to learn English, so while you're helping them build a playground, or helping in a kindergarten class, you'll be meeting Czech students your own age. As with most community service programs, the accommodations are austere. You won't be staying in any four-star hotels. You will most likely live in a student residence of some kind. But for a few days during the trip, you'll stay with a Czech family, and they will take you around the town in which you will be working.

The last five days are spent in Prague, one of the most beautiful cities on the planet.

 Kristen Olsen, from Colorado, went on the Putney Seeds for Progress trip to Costa Rica. The program was "in a very, very small little village. I don't even think I would call it a village." Although they were warned about the harsh living conditions and were told to bring rain jackets and shovels, none of the participants were prepared for the rustic living conditions they found there:

"We were in the middle of this rain forest. It was actually called a humid forest. It rained all the time and it was muddy. We had two houses, one for the boys and one for the girls. Well, they weren't really houses, they were actually shacks. We slept like sardines. If I turned over, I would be on the person next to me. It smelled like our house was over a septic tank." She also pointed out that the moisture was almost unbearable: "The worst part was living in the rainy weather. It was gloomy and rainy all the time. It was so moist there that you couldn't wash your clothes. And if you were lucky they would dry in a few weeks. And after they dried, they still smelled mildewy."

The team worked together building a park in the little village. "We had to dig a lot to lay the cement. It was a lot of tedious and hard labor that didn't seem to amount to much. But in the end, it actually turned out really well. We built a whole park. It was nice. The village didn't really have a central place for everyone to meet. So the park became the town center."

The experience was great. The whole group learned to laugh at adversity, and every weekend, Putney had planned great excursions to beaches and towns. Even the lowest point of the trip, when the toilets overflowed and soiled the sleeping bags, became a good anecdote. The entire group laughed about it.

As you might imagine, to go on a trip like this requires a positive attitude. You need to be able to try new things and see the bright side of anything. And you have to look at the trip like an adventure, one that you need to take an active part in enjoying. If Olsen has one piece of advice to give to a future participant it's to make the most of the experience: "The most fun that I had was when I didn't really care about anything. Part of the beauty of it all was I didn't care how I looked or what I wore. You've got to take that hike even if you're tired, or jump in the water with your clothes on. Take that extra leap."

Visions

Address R.D. #3, Box 106B, Newport, PA 17074

Phone (717) 567-7313

Fax (717) 567-7853

Cost $2,180–$3,080 (Travel to and from starting point not included. Financial aid deadline is February 15.)

Ages 14–18

Size of group Fewer than 25 people per group with 6 staff members

Length of program 21–35 days

Application deadline Early applications are preferred. Applications are processed in the order in which they are received.

Description A program of community service and cross-cultural communication in Alaska, Appalachia, Montana, and the Caribbean.

Summary A chance to travel and effect change through community service. Only for those who are mature and willing to live in a different culture.

History Visions is a nonprofit, nonsectarian program that offers community service trips for high school students. In August 1994, it was chosen as an AmeriCorps program, a high honor for any volunteer organization. A Visions program is not for the squeamish. You will be living in an environment that you might find more challenging than any you have experienced.

The Program On any given Visions trip, you will be spending roughly 60 percent of your time engaged in community service. In the Visions program in Montana, this means that you will most likely be engaged in some type of construction. You will stay on one of four Indian reservations, and you will spend a lot of time with the locals. In addition to the community work that you do, you will get to experience living in a different culture. You will meet with your leaders four evenings a week, to discuss all the great experiences you're having.

A Visions program is not all about learning, however; you will also spend much of your time exploring the beautiful Montana countryside. When you aren't working, you can go white-water rafting, climb rocks, ride horses, or hike in nearby national and state parks. If you go on one of these programs, you will be challenged. Make sure you're ready to experience some of the privations that the people you're helping live with every day.

In addition, you will learn a great deal about yourself. The counselors and the owners really believe that helping people can be a spiritually uplifting experience that teaches you new things. One of their trips is an excellent chance to try new things and learn about yourself.

 Sarah Bookbinder of Newton, Massachusetts went with Visions to Montana where she lived on the Crow reservation. She really liked the trip. "The best thing about it is it's really exciting because you get to do challenging things like hiking and stuff; you get to experience another culture; and you get to help them out. We built a playground. The program gives you an outlook that the country is really different, that it's not just the East Coast."

She was especially pleased with how well the program was organized: "The program is run so well. The counselors are unbelievable. You totally feel like they just care about you so much. I think everyone on the trip just grows so much. They grow from more than the specific activities, they grow from being around different people."

One memory that sticks in her mind is when they went into a sweat lodge: "We did all these cultural things. We did a sweat lodge, which is a little hut (it's an Indian tradition). They put these boiling rocks in, and it's covered in smoke. You go in with no clothes (it's single-sex). You go in and get drenched in sweat. It's kind of like an out-of-body experience. It's painful, but it's the most rewarding thing. And when you come out you have the most unbelievable high that you can ever imagine. A lot of kids have never really seriously prayed before. It gives you an unique experience to get an inner look at your-self."

While her Visions trip was excellent, she doesn't think it is for everyone: "You'd like to think that everyone should go on this trip, but you really have to want to try. You don't have to be an experienced hiker or an experienced builder. You just have to want a new experience and be open-minded."

If you go on the trip, she advises that you "try as many new things as you can. This is probably the one chance you will get to do something like this. When you get back you'll realize that it's such an incredible advantage that you should take as much advantage of it as you can."

World Horizons

Address P.O. Box 662, Bethlehem, CT 06751

Phone (800) 262-5874; (203) 262-5874

Cost $3,300–$3,840 (Round-trip airfare from NYC included. Limited financial aid is available based on need.)

Ages 15–18 (Participants for the more popular trips are grouped by age.)

Size of group About 10 people per group with one instructor

Length of program 28–35 days

Application deadline Early applications are preferred. Applications are processed in the order in which they are received.

Description World Horizons is a community service program that sends participants to the Caribbean, Central America, South America, Samoa, Alaska, and Southern Africa. You will travel in small groups and help out in needy communities.

Summary World Horizons allows you to help people and experience a great deal of their culture. You will participate in group projects, some of which you initiate.

History The director of World Horizons founded the company in 1987 and has an additional eighteen years of experience directing a similar cross-cultural program. World Horizons makes a huge effort to give you the experience of living within the culture that you're visiting. Although difficult, the experience will be enriching, and you will leave with a better sense of yourself and your community than you ever had before.

The Program The typical World Horizons program is not luxurious. You'll be staying in simple housing characteristic of the community. On the World Horizons trip to Western Samoa, you'll live in a fale, an open-sided thatched roof home, and you'll wear the traditional lava-lava dress that the local people wear. The work you do will involve fixing up buildings and organizing a day camp.

You will spend much of your time with your group, but you will also get to know some of the local people—especially the kids—who will be fascinated with meeting someone from as far off as America. If you're willing to actively work at meeting people, you'll learn a different perspective from the one you're used to.

The work, while not easy, won't be too demanding, and you'll have some time to hang out with the group and the local people. By the time you finish, you'll have done a difficult but rewarding service for the local people, and become much more knowledgeable about the state of the world today.

Conclusion

After researching all these programs and activities, we were left with one overriding conclusion: there's too much to choose from to allow yourself to sit around the house and watch MTV all day. Get out there and do something this summer. Not only will you end up with something cool to tell your friends, but you'll have great memories long after your tan line fades and the lifeguard stands are taken down. Not to be a downer, but unless you're tremendously lucky and become independently wealthy, the next few years will really be the only time you'll have to be so free and breezy. Soon, you'll be on to bigger and better things that take up a lot more of your time (but we can talk about that some other day). Have an adventure, become a bottomless pit of movie trivia or an expert on American landscape painting. Whatever. Wherever. Just do what it takes to make it happen.

We hope that this book will help you in your search for a fantastic summer. You're only going to be a teenager once. You might as well do it right.

ABOUT THE AUTHOR

Michael Freedman has written and taught for The Princeton Review for many years. Michael lives in Brooklyn with two cats, his wife Grace, and their brand new son, Jacob. This is his third book for The Princeton Review.

NOTES

NOTES

NOTES

NOTES

NOTES

CULTURESCOPE

The ———— Princeton Review
Guide to an Informed Mind

Has this ever happened to you?

You're at a party. An attractive person whom you have been dying to meet comes over and says, "Man, does that woman have a Joan of Arc complex, or what?" and you, in a tone that is most suave, say "Uh," while your mind races wildly, "*Joan of Arc, OK, France, uh...damn,*" as the aforementioned attractive person smiles weakly and heads for the punch bowl.

No? How about this?

Your boss finally learns your name and says, "Ah, good to have you aboard. Do you like Renaissance painting?" You reply with an emphatic "Yes! I do!" to which she returns, "What's your favorite fresco?" You start stammering, glassy-eyed, your big moment passing you by as visions of soda pop dance through your brain.

CULTURESCOPE can help.

If you have gaps of knowledge big enough to drive an eighteen-wheeler through, The Princeton Review has the thing for you. It's called CULTURESCOPE. It's a book that can make people think you've read enough books to fill a semi, even if you haven't.

CULTURESCOPE covers everything: history, science, math, art, sports, geography, popular culture—it's all in there, and it's fun, because along with all of the great information there are quizzes, resource lists, fun statistics, wacky charts, and lots of pretty pictures.

In bookstores now.

You won't go away empty-headed.

THE
PRINCETON
REVIEW

THE PRINCETON REVIEW WORLDWIDE

Each year, thousands of students from countries throughout the world prepare for the TOEFL and for U.S. college and graduate school admissions exams. Whether you plan to prepare for your exams in your home country or the United States, The Princeton Review is committed to your success.

INTERNATIONAL LOCATIONS: If you are using our books outside of the United States and have questions or comments, or want to know if our courses are being offered in your area, be sure to contact the Princeton Review office nearest you:

- HONG KONG   852-517-3016
- JAPAN (Tokyo)   8133-463-1343
- KOREA (Seoul)   822-795-3028
- MEXICO CITY   011-525-358-0855
- MONTREAL   617-558-2828 (a U.S. based number)
- PAKISTAN (Lahore)   92-42-872-315
- SAUDI ARABIA   413-548-6849 (a U.S. based number)
- SPAIN (Madrid)   341-446-5541
- TAIWAN (Taipei)   886-27511293

U.S. STUDY ABROAD: *Review USA* offers international students many advantages and opportunities. In addition to helping you gain acceptance to the U.S. college or university of your choice, *Review USA* will help you acquire the knowledge and orientation you need to succeed once you get there.

Review USA is unique. It includes supplements to your test-preparation courses and a special series of *AmeriCulture* workshops to prepare you for the academic rigors and student life in the United States. Our workshops are designed to familiarize you with the different U.S. expressions, real-life vocabulary, and cultural challenges you will encounter as a study-abroad student. While studying with us, you'll make new friends and have the opportunity to personally visit college and university campuses to determine which school is right for you.

Whether you are planning to take the TOEFL, SAT, GRE, GMAT, LSAT, MCAT, or USMLE exam, The Princeton Review's test preparation courses, expert instructors, and dedicated International Student Advisors can help you achieve your goals.

For additional information about *Review USA*, admissions requirements, class schedules, F-1 visas, I-20 documentation, and course locations, write to:

The Princeton Review • Review USA

2315 Broadway, New York NY 10024

Fax: 212/874-0775